Everyday Miracles

Sixty-Four Stories of God's Love and Power

Sherry Evans

Everyday Miracles
Copyright © 2016 Sherry Evans
All rights reserved.
ISBN-13: 978-1539464341

All Rights Reserved. No part of this publication may be reproduced, stored in a retrieval system or transmitted in any form or by any means – online, electronic, mechanical, photocopy, recording or any other – except for brief quotations in printed reviews, without prior permission of the author.

All Scripture quotations, unless otherwise specified, are from the King James Version of the Bible (Copyright © 1977, 1984, Thomas Nelson Inc., Publishers.)

Table of Contents

Introduction 1
Online Miracles 5
    My Journey - Is There Not a Cause? 6
    It Is Saturday Night, but Monday Is Coming 9
    Burning Foot 12
    The Big One 15
    Let the Children Come 18
    The Little Boy Who Walked 21
    From Housebound to the Pulpit 25
    No Room for the Both of Us 29
    The New Fit 31
    I'm Confused! 33
    Happy Tears 37
    Wrestling with God 40
    "Of Whom the World Was Not Worthy" 44
    You May Go Home 47
    Six Hundred Pounds versus God 49

These Things Don't Just Disappear 51
Here Today, Gone Tomorrow 53
The Good Little Jewish Girl 55
Laughter Is Good Medicine 58
Jumping for Joy 60
Voodoo 62
Supernatural Expansion 65

Miracles in the Marketplace 69
My Journey - The Threefold Cord of Healing 70
The Shaking Man 74
Sammy 76
Jesus' Power Trumps New Age 79
Kept Alive by a Dream 82
Out of the Hospital and into God's Healing 85
The Sinner Woman 88
The Man Who Had Died 91
The Transvestite 94
Funny You Should Ask 96
I'm Going to Kill Myself Tonight 99
I'm Not Religious Either 102

Miracles in Services 105
My Journey - If You Don't Go… 106
The Little Boy Who Couldn't Get Enough 108

No Language Barrier with God 111
Perfect People Not Required... 114
The Same God… 116
Going to Church to Get Healed 119
I Feel Hands around My Neck 122
Herniated Disc and Spirit of
Grief Gone 126
I Want to See Cancer Healed... 129
Led by a Word and a Vision 132
Never Too Old 135
I-I-I Don't Know Why I'm Shaking............................... 137
The Case of the Mistaken Diagnosis 140
The Ten-Year-Long Migraine... 144
The Lady in Red 147
The Strange Case of Numbness 150
The "Walking Time Bomb".. 153
The Healing Seed 156
The Four for One Miracle 159
The Unclaimed Word of Knowledge 161
Unstuck!... 164
The Little Girl with Braids... 167
I Feel Your Hand... 169
Miracles Are Contagious 171

Tears of Joy	173
How Many Years?	176
Miscellaneous Miracles	**181**
My Journey - Faithfulness Is Key	182
An Amish Man and a Christmas Miracle	185
Pain-free, Limp-free, Impediment-free	188
I'm Walking without Pain!	190
Hot Flashes, the Miracle Dog, and the "Drunk" Man	192
Tingling in the Brain	195
The Persistent Mother (AKA Mama Bear) and the Prodigal Son	197
The "Spring Chicken"	203
Ministering Healing	**207**
The Practical Side	208
Developing a Culture for the Supernatural Church	213
Pick up Your Shoes	219
Prayer for Healing	222
About The Author	223

Introduction

I remember sitting in a church service years ago watching a healing evangelist minister to the sick. Something inside of my spirit was ignited, and in my heart I cried out, "Lord, I have to do that too." Unfortunately, it was many years before I began to do what my heart cried out to do.

I spent much time repeatedly asking the Lord how I could make a difference while I was on Earth. For many years, I did not receive an answer. However, the Lord answered my desperate plea for guidance during a week of special meetings. For that week, we had a healing evangelist at our church named Roger Webb, and, as I watched him, my hunger and desire to see the sick healed was reignited in a powerful way. I realized that the answer to my desires to make a difference on this earth was written in the Bible all along. We are already told to preach the gospel, heal the sick, and to set the captives free.

I began to pray for the sick in my own church first, and then I expanded my healing ministry to people on Facebook chat. As I did so, I had an opportunity to learn and grow in the comfort of my own home. Many of the testimonies that I share in this book are from those days. Eventually, I began to minister at healing services of my own. God gave me the desire of my heart. Pay attention to your deep desires. In the majority of cases, God put them there.

As I began to minister to the sick, I had to overcome much wrong thinking. I would often pray, "Lord, is it Your will for me to pray for the sick? What if I have the wrong motives?" The Holy Spirit was truly faithful to answer those questions. Some of the teaching came directly from Him, and some of it came from several mentors who spoke into my life. Because of these early questions, I understand the struggles that others have as they get started in the same type of ministry.

In these stories, you will read of many of my mistakes and the faithfulness of God in spite of my mistakes. You will read of times when God went far beyond my understanding to minister to needs that I knew nothing about. You will read of times when I heard God's direction and times when I struggled to know God's direction. You will encounter His extravagant love for people and His indescribable sense of humor. You will see that our weaknesses will not stop His work going forth as we are willing to simply step out and do as His Word commands.

I have written this book for two groups of people—those needing healing and those wanting to minister in the area of healing. I desire this to be a book of hope for both groups.

For those who need healing, I give you Jesus. He loves you very much and sees the pain and struggles that you face every day. Even though it is good to receive prayer from others, do not look at any healing minister as your answer. Instead, look to the Lord. Jesus healed all who came to Him. Immerse yourself in the stories of Jesus as He healed the multitudes. Picture yourself in the crowds. He would not have passed you by. Focus on Him and never give up. Hold on to the promises in the Word with all that you have, and, at the same time, rest in Him. I pray that, as you read these stories, the power of God will come on you and set you free from every sickness and disease.

For those who desire to minister healing, I give you Jesus as well. Remember that He lives inside of you and desires to touch and heal people through you. As you begin to lay hands on the sick and expect them to recover, the Holy Spirit will personally mentor you. Your faith will grow as you obey. Certainly, the enemy will try to talk you into quitting. Resist him. Just like you, I am on a journey of growth in the area of healing. I do not see everyone I pray for healed, but I believe that someday I will. I pray that these stories encourage you to take a leap of faith. I desire that you will be encouraged and challenged to step into this life of adventure.

We are entering a time when the work of God is accelerating. A visionary encounter that I had years ago demonstrates this acceleration. In my vision, I saw a catalogue with all types of medical equipment. Then, in a second, I saw a seeing-eye dog. I was confused, and asked, "Lord, why are YOU showing me these things?"

He answered, "I am showing you this because someday these things will be unnecessary. I want you to position yourself for that day." The Lord was not saying that the use of any of those things is wrong, but He was saying that our capacity to walk in the power of God will grow until we see masses of people set free and healed.

I asked God the next logical question: "How do I position myself to be a part of this?"

He answered, "Remain humble, remain hungry, and remain faithful."

It's time!

Online Miracles

My Journey - Is There Not a Cause?

When I began praying for the sick, I took a few hours every night to minister healing on Facebook. Amazingly, I had many conflicting emotions about this ministry. Satan was busy whispering lies in my mind to try to stop me from reaching people in this way.

One of the questions that I persistently had was in the area of motives. Were my motives pure? Was there any possibility that I was only praying for people in order to gain attention? Of course, it is important to minister out of love for people and love for God, but if the enemy can cause us to be overly introspective concerning our motives, he will. It will become another distraction that hinders us and may eventually stop us altogether.

One evening, this question about motives was especially bothering me. I posted on my Facebook status an honest question: "How do you know if you have the correct motives in ministry?" As would be expected, I received an abundance of answers to that question. As I read them, I became more confused than before I posted the question.

Soon afterwards, I posted my usual evening status: "If you are sick or in pain, meet me in Facebook chat for prayer." I was quickly inundated with chat windows popping up and people asking for healing. I was so busy that I forgot my concern about motives.

Suddenly, I heard the clear voice of the Holy Spirit speaking to me. He interrupted my ministry with an urgent message. He said, "Is there not a cause?" The Lord really had my attention then because I knew where that phrase was located in the Bible.

David's father told David to take food to his brothers who were in battle. (I Samuel 17) David set out with the food, but when he got there, he was shocked. Goliath had terrorized the troops that were cowering before him. The giant was asking for a champion to fight him, but not one soldier was willing. Fear was reigning over them all.

David overheard the men speaking of a great reward for the man who would go to battle against Goliath. He thought he heard of a reward that included wealth, the king's daughter, and freedom for his family. His ears perked up, and he asked, "What is going to be done for the one who kills this Philistine and takes away the reproach from Israel?"

David's oldest brother, Eliab, heard David's words and became offended. Most likely, he felt guilty for not being willing to fight Goliath himself. He turned to David and sneered, "Who did you leave those few sheep with? I know the naughtiness of your heart. You just came to see the battle." Eliab questioned David's motives.

David defended himself, saying, "What have I done? Is there not a cause?"

God spoke to me loud and clear that night. There is a great cause. People are suffering and dying. These questions about motives did not come from Him. There was an enemy that wanted to stop me in my tracks so that I would not set the captives free. I repented quickly and put my questions and fears aside.

The next morning, I woke up to an amazing message. A woman wrote, "I believe I have the word of the Lord for you. It is not the time to worry about motives. There is a real giant out there, and you have what it takes to bring it down." God confirmed what He had spoken to me the night before.

When you decide to reach out to others and minister healing, salvation, or deliverance, someone will always question your motives. Just as Eliab was motivated by guilt and jealousy, others may be motivated in the same way. Instead of dealing with their own fear, they may attack you.

Satan may also cause you to question your motives. He does not want you to destroy his works in people's lives. If he can keep you in confusion, he will certainly do that.

The good news is that God is able to bring correction to any wrong motive as you continue to minister. Move with the love of God, but don't allow intimidation from the enemy stop you. There is a giant out there—it is a giant of sickness and disease. However, the Healer lives inside of you. Allow Him to heal through you.

It Is Saturday Night, but Monday Is Coming

I have often said that when the hunger is great enough, you will find a way. I have lived that truth in my own life in the area of healing. Because my husband and I were pastors of a small church, my ferocious desire to minister healing sometimes felt unsatisfied. There simply were not enough people in our church with the need for healing. Especially during the long Ohio winters when I spent much time indoors, I wanted another way to pray for the sick.

A solution to my hunger came when I heard that a healing evangelist, Roger Webb, was praying for people over Facebook chat. The results were amazing as miracles seemed to occur on a nightly basis. Shortly after that, Roger encouraged me to minister in a similar way. Because of my hunger, I jumped at the opportunity. I began to post in my status a simple invitation for people who needed healing to contact me through chat. To my great amazement, I began to see people healed over chat as Roger had. It is possible that this is one of the "greater works" that Jesus talked about that all believers could do. (John 14:12) Jesus could not pray for people who lived on the other side of the world when He was on Earth, but because of technology, we can.

It was late on a Saturday night when I received a message on Facebook. A woman wrote, "I am in horrible pain right now. Would you pray for me?" I asked her what was causing the pain, and she told me that the pain was coming from a tumor on her spine. I hate cancer, so I began to pray for her with quite a bit of emotion. As I prayed, I reminded this woman, myself, and the Lord that Jesus had already paid for her healing. Then I commanded the tumor to go, as well as the pain from the tumor.

I asked, "How is the pain now?" It would be wonderful to say that the pain instantly left, but it did not. I persisted for a while and finally decided to call it a night. Because of my lack of experience at that time, I was quite disappointed. In spite of my discouragement, I encouraged her to continue to believe for the manifestation of her healing and I would do the same. II Corinthians 5:7 tells us that we walk by faith, not by sight. This walk of faith is extremely important in healing. I thought about this woman often the next day. Oh, how I wanted her to be healed.

I woke up on Monday morning without thinking of this woman with the tumor. I did not yet know the great miracle that God had performed. When I opened up my Facebook page, I saw that I had received a new message from her. With curiosity, I opened her message and what she wrote made my day. She said, "Guess what. The prayers worked. I had a new scan today, and the tumor is gone! It is really gone!"

I felt as if my heart would beat out of my chest because of the joy that I experienced for her. I felt like a little girl gazing with wonder at her great and powerful father. Father God had performed a miracle for the woman that He loved so dearly. He is truly awesome. Sometime between Saturday night and Monday morning, God had removed the tumor.

Burning Foot

Human beings have an innate desire for adventure and romance. We see it illustrated in the movies and television programs that people watch. God put those desires in us. He wants us to fulfill those desires in our relationship with Him. The deepest love relationship we can have is with the King of the Universe, Jesus Christ. The greatest adventures that we can experience come as we co-labor with the Holy Spirit to see people set free from the oppression of the enemy. Instead of meeting our needs for adventure and romance through the medium of entertainment, we can meet those needs in our actual lives. We can walk through this world as one with the Person who adores us while destroying the works of the devil. I have found healing to be a wonderful adventure that the Lord and I go on together. He often surprises me in what He does and how He does it. He knows people better than I do, and He knows what they need.

One evening, I received a message on Facebook from a woman who wanted prayer for inner healing. Even though there is no formula for healing of emotions, when I receive that kind of request, I will normally encourage the person to give the entire situation to the Lord. I ask Him to heal their heart, and then I command any demonic spirits involved with the inner hurt to go. Finally, I release the peace, love, and joy of the Holy Spirit.

As I was praying in this way, the woman said to me, "My foot is burning!" I had not been praying for her foot at all when this happened, and she had not mentioned a problem with her foot. *What is God up to now?* I thought.

I asked her, "Was there something wrong with your foot?"

She told me, "I have not had an arch in that foot for many years. I have been in much pain because of it." I smiled to myself as I thought about how amazing God is.

It is important to follow the lead of the Holy Spirit, so I prayed in cooperation with what He was already doing. I typed, "In Jesus' name, I command an arch to form in that flat foot."

I asked her, "What's happening now?"

She repeated, "My foot is still burning." After I prayed for her a few more times, I pronounced a blessing over her night's sleep and got offline. I gave the situation to the Lord and went to sleep as well. I didn't give it another thought.

The next day, I got a message from her again. She wrote, "It was so strange. I kept waking up all night long, and each time I woke up, my foot was still burning. Something amazing happened. When I checked my foot in the morning, there was a perfect arch in it!"

God knew what she needed even when I didn't. His compassion is so great that He met that need without my understanding of it. I have learned to trust Him each time I pray for someone. Proverbs 3:5 instructs us, "Trust in the Lord with all your heart and do not lean unto your own understanding." He is the God who loves to surprise us.

"Now to Him who is able to do exceedingly, abundantly more than we can ask or think, according to the power that works within us, to Him be glory in the church by Christ Jesus throughout all ages, forever. Amen." (Ephesians 3:20, 21)

The Big One

When I awoke one morning, I noticed a Facebook message on my phone. Although I receive a lot of Facebook messages, when I opened this one, I realized that the need was urgent. The woman who wrote the message explained, "I'm in an emergency situation. I have had two strokes in the last two weeks. My doctor said that I have to have surgery as soon as possible. I need a miracle. Will you pray for me?"

I asked with some concern, "Do you know what caused the strokes?" For many people, the answer to that may have been obvious, but I know little about medical issues.

She answered, "The strokes were caused by two blocked arteries. My doctor told me that the next stroke could be 'the big one'. It could be devastating to my body." Naturally, she felt a great deal of fear about this.

After speaking to her for a few minutes about God's healing power, I commanded the blockages in her arteries to dissolve. Afterwards, she wrote, "I feel tingling all over my body!"

This is always a good sign when praying for healing, and I felt joy welling up inside. I told her, "God is healing you." I was probably more excited than she was.

Healing power is often felt as heat or tingling. Less often, a person may feel cold, numbness or pressure. Sometimes a person is healed without feeling anything at all.

After I prayed for her physical healing, I prayed that God's peace would come upon her. She replied, "My whole body relaxed as you prayed. I feel such peace."

Peace is a common experience when a person receives prayer because Jesus is the Prince of Peace. For many, this peace is the best part of the healing experience.

Because I pray for so many people, I forgot all about this woman and her need. It is comforting to know that when I forget, God does not.

When I heard from her the next time, the fear was gone and had been replaced with joy. She had gone to a follow-up visit with her surgeon, and he decided to do new testing. After the tests were over, the surgeon walked into the room where she was waiting and held up the new test results. He said, "Ma'am, I don't know how it happened, but the blockages are no longer there."

After she got over the shock at this turn of events, she asked about the surgery. He simply told her, "Surgery is cancelled." God had prevented the possibility of another stroke—possibly "the big one".

EVERYDAY MIRACLES

When you minister in the area of healing, there are disappointments in which a person does not seem to receive their much needed healing, but one cancelled surgery or one person healed of debilitating pain and injury makes healing ministry worth every minute of it.

Let the Children Come

I love to pray for children. They believe so easily, and they can be depended on to be honest about what they are experiencing during prayer. When I am speaking to a child who needs healing, I will often ask, "How many children do you think Jesus healed when He prayed for everyone in the multitudes?" Then I answer, "He probably healed hundreds and hundreds of children just like you." They usually respond with a big smile and a nod of their heads. Since even children can have dental issues, I have prayed for a number of them with different types of problems with their teeth. Three of these situations stand out in my mind.

In one case, a father sent me a message on Facebook explaining that his three-year-old daughter had multiple cavities. Since she could not read my prayer, I asked him to hold his daughter on his lap and read the prayer that I typed aloud to her. The father did just that. Since she did not have any pain, the father did not know the results right away.

Shortly after that, the father took his daughter to the dentist. After the visit, he wrote, "Thank you so much for praying for my daughter. The cavities are all gone. God is so wonderful!"

On another occasion, I received an email from a woman who told me an unusual story. She had read a blog that I had written for Spirit Fuel, an online prophetic and inspirational website. This particular blog was about dental miracles. At the end of the article, I had posted a prayer for healing for dental issues. This is what the prayer said: "Lord, right now, cause Your power and Your fire to go through mouths, teeth, and gums. Give each person reading this a dental miracle. In Jesus' name, I speak to pain to go, cavities to be filled, jaws to line up, and for teeth to grow back. Thank you, Lord. In Jesus' name, amen."

This woman had several children with cavities in their teeth. She quickly lined them up and read the prayer that I had posted word for word to them. She wrote, "I knew that God would heal my children and agreed with the words that you prayed. When I took them back to the dentist for a follow-up visit, he told me that every single cavity was gone from my children's teeth. God is so faithful!"

In another situation, a mother sent me a message on Facebook explaining, "My eleven-year-old daughter has a terrible toothache."

I asked, "Do you know what is causing the toothache?

She answered, "Yes. She has a cracked tooth."

I commanded the pain to go and the tooth itself to be healed. After several prayers and commands, the pain was gone.

Several days later, the mother sent me another message. She said, "My daughter can't find the crack anymore at all. It is gone! She keeps rubbing her tongue around that tooth, and there is no crack. My daughter is amazed. She saw the power of God in her life in a tangible way."

Jesus took time for the children when He was on Earth. He cared about their needs and desired to bless them. He has not changed. He longs to touch the littlest child with His love and power. When children experience a miracle, they will never forget the event. They will be marked with the knowledge that God is real and that He loves them.

The Little Boy Who Walked

Miracles involving children are especially precious to me. I can imagine Jesus taking a child in His arms and healing them because of His deep love for them. A beautiful example of God's compassion for a child took place not too long ago.

A precious woman contacted me on Facebook messages one evening asking for prayer for her two-year-old son. He had fallen and had hurt his ankle in some way, but because he was nonverbal, he could not tell her the location of the pain. His mother had taken him to the doctor earlier, but the doctor preferred to wait and see if the pain would resolve on its own rather than have the boy receive an x-ray.

As I often do with children who cannot read, I asked the mother to hold her son while I prayed for him. I further told her to read my prayer to her son as I typed it. After I commanded healing, the mother took her son and put him on his feet. Sadly, she said, "He is screaming in pain."

Many times repeated prayers bring the miracle, so I prayed again. Once more, she put him on his feet, and he screamed. She had no intentions of giving up, however. The mother had a strong faith and determination that her son would be healed, so I prayed again. This time, she said, "His ankle is hot, and he is kicking his leg up and down." I suggested to her that she wait until the heat was gone before she put him on his feet again, and she agreed to do that. Later that evening, she sent me another message and said, "He is not crying or screaming when I put him on his feet now. Thank you for praying."

The next day, she sent me another message, but this message reflected a new joy and excitement. She wrote, "He is healed! In fact, he is using his legs like he never has before!" Because I did not know the entire story, I did not yet understand why she was so excited. There was a very significant part of this testimony that I did not yet understand, but I was soon to find out. God went far beyond my expectation.

Two days after I had prayed for the little boy, his mother sent me another message, along with a video of her son walking. I watched the little boy walking around, and thought, *He is so cute*. However, I did not see the importance of it—not until she explained it to me. She said, "He is walking all around the house even though two days ago he could not walk at all. He had even stopped standing up. In fact, he wouldn't even sit up in his stroller. We had to carry him everywhere we went. God has healed my son!"

I asked, "What? He couldn't walk at all before?"

The mother said, "No, he couldn't walk at all."

The mother explained to me that her son had stopped progressing in his development at six months of age. The doctors had ordered a brain scan and found that there was damage to his brain. However, the doctors could offer no explanation as to why this had happened. They were also concerned about a defective gene that he carried. Eleven months before the day I prayed, the doctors had told his mother that he might live his life in a vegetative state. They also believed that he was blind and would never see. They were certain that he would never walk. The medical field could not help.

Before the mother had become a Christian, she had sought out several idols to heal her son, but there were no results. Of course this would be true because an idol is nothing. However, Jesus is alive. He is still healing, saving, and setting people free. He paid for all of these things when He went to the cross and the whipping post for us.

The Lord heard the desperate cry of a loving mother. He honored her faith and persistence and gave her son a great miracle. She had persistently asked others to pray for him, and she had spent much time in the Word building up her faith for his healing. Several days before he was healed, she had told a friend that he would walk. In fact, she insisted that he would walk. She said this before he had taken his first step. He is now walking all over the house. On top of that, his eyesight is now excellent.

Shortly after the little boy's healing, a physical therapist came to visit. In amazement, the physical therapist told the mother that they would no longer need her services. The boy was healed.

I saw one more video of this little boy. In it, he was dancing all over his church. I know that Jesus was smiling in delight.

I thought that I was praying for the healing of a physical but temporary injury, but God went much further than that. He jumpstarted the young boy's development and gave him the precious gift of mobility.

From Housebound to the Pulpit

One night, I was praying for people on a healing chat program called "Faith for Healing in Jesus' Name" when I received a disturbing message. A man wrote, "I'm killing myself tonight. I can't go on."

Concerned, I asked him, "Do you have a plan?"

He answered, "Yes, I have a gun right beside me." I knew that if he already had a plan in place, he was quite serious. I also knew that he still hoped for freedom or he would not have come on the chat program.

I continued to draw him out by asking him questions about his life. I asked, "What is so difficult that you no longer want to live?"

He answered, "I'm addicted to anxiety and depression medicine, but I'm still anxious and depressed. I can't even leave my house because of the social anxiety I deal with. I can't live with this any longer."

I asked the Holy Spirit for wisdom and the words to say to this man. I knew that this situation was bigger than me, but God had the answers.

Then I typed, "God loves you so much. Jesus paid the price for your salvation and for your freedom. He can set you free. There is still hope, and God is waiting for you with open arms. You can have peace again." As I typed, I prayed that God would completely set him free that night. It was urgent.

I continued to pray that the Lord would draw this man to Himself and asked, "Are you ready to invite Jesus to come into your life?"

"Yes, I am," he said. I led him in a prayer in which he surrendered his life to the Lord and in which he received God's gift of eternal life. Then I began to speak to the spirits of anxiety and depression to go. I broke the power of those things off of his life. I He asked me to pray that he could stop smoking so I commanded any spirit of addiction to leave as well.

It was not long before he said, "I feel so light. It is all gone! The depression and the anxiety are gone!" I felt elated at what God had done for this man. God did in an instant what years of counseling did not do for him. I also realized that he was going to need follow-up help in his new life.

I asked where he lived and quickly searched the internet for a good church. I found a wonderful, Spirit-filled church that looked as if it would meet his needs. He quickly located the website online as well.

They were having a service that night, and, without a word from me, he said, "I'm going to go to church tonight." I could hardly believe what I was hearing. I knew a miracle had taken place for him to desire to go to a large church alone. The social anxiety was gone.

During the weeks that followed, I often thought of this man, and I continued to pray for him. I knew that many people face a ferocious battle to stay free even after God sets them free. I did not have a way to reach him again, and so I wondered how he was doing. When I finally heard from him again, I was not disappointed.

About a month later, he again entered the Faith for Healing chat program. I was so excited to hear from him. He said, "I have never had to take another pill for anxiety or depression. I did not go through withdrawal symptoms from stopping them so suddenly either. I have not smoked another cigarette. You saved my life!"

I said, "It was the Lord who saved your life. He loves you so much."

He continued to tell me that he was still attending the church he visited the night he got saved. "Not only that," he excitedly said, "but I am a part of three small groups, one of which I am teaching. This Sunday, I am going to share my testimony in front of the entire church." The man who formerly could not even leave his house because of social anxiety was going to be speaking in front of hundreds of people. Only God could set a man free so completely. What an awesome God!

God is not only able to heal physically, He is also able to heal emotionally. Sometimes counseling is helpful, but one touch from the Lord can bypass years of counseling. God is able to do what no man can. Isaiah 53:5 tells us, "But He (Jesus) was pierced for our transgressions, he was crushed for our iniquities, the punishment that brought us peace was upon Him, and by His wounds we are healed." Jesus paid a price so that you can be free from fear. He paid for your peace. Put your trust in Him. Spend time in His presence. Attend services where the power of God is flowing. He will set you free.

No Room for the Both of Us

Women who become pregnant can experience intense, but mixed emotions. This can be true for any pregnant mother, but the emotional "roller coaster" can be more extreme for a woman who has a health issue that could endanger her child. One morning, I received a message on Facebook from a woman who was on that "roller coaster". She had recently discovered that she was pregnant, but her doctor had also told her that, along with the baby, there was a tumor in her uterus that could endanger her child's life. Her message went from exuberant joy to deep concern. On top of that, the tumor was causing her uterus to lean to one side and to push against her bladder. The result of the intruding tumor was much pain and many bladder infections.

There are times when I feel compassion for the sick, but at other times I feel anger—anger against the enemy for the way he tries to oppress people. This was a day on which I felt anger. I remembered that Matthew 21:21 says, "…if you have faith and do not doubt, you shall not only do what has been done to this fig tree, but you shall say to this mountain, 'be moved and be thrown into the sea,' and it shall be done." I knew that if I could speak to a mountain and it would move then I could speak to a tumor and it would go.

With much emotion, I commanded, "Tumor, shrink and go from her uterus in Jesus' name."

As I spoke to the tumor, she interrupted me and wrote, "I feel tingling! Wow! I feel things moving around in there!" Tingling is always a good thing when you are praying for the sick, so I prayed a few more times that God would increase His power in her body. I asked her to tell me how she felt when the tingling was gone. She waited a few moments, and then she told me, "The uncomfortable feeling in my bladder is completely gone! Praise God!"

I was thankful that the woman was no longer in pain, and I believed that she had received her miracle. However, I never report that someone is healed simply when the pain leaves. Instead, I wait for documentation from a doctor or hospital.

About a week later, I received another message from her. I eagerly opened it up as my heart cried out for a good report for her and her baby. She explained that she had been to the hospital for a new scan. The excitement in the words that she wrote to me was contagious. She wrote, "It's gone! The tumor is gone! On top of that, the uterus is back in place right where it should be, and the baby is healthy and well!"

I consider it the greatest honor to see a miracle such as that one. The good news is that anyone can see miracles. When you begin to step out in obedience to the Word, the Lord will work with you.

The New Fit

Many times I will pray for someone's physical issue without knowing or understanding the cause of that physical issue. I often know little about the disease or disability itself. However, God does know, and He understands how to bring the healing. He works beyond my limited knowledge. All He needs is faith in His ability and willingness to heal.

One evening, a woman sent me a message on Facebook telling me that she had extreme tooth pain because the enamel on her molars was worn away. I did not know what could cause that to happen, but I put all my faith in Jesus. I commanded, "Teeth, be healed, and, pain, go from her mouth in Jesus' name."

After several commands and prayers, she said, "The pain is gone!" She was thrilled and went to bed a happy woman. I also went to bed feeling grateful for what God had done. Neither of us knew that the best was yet to come.

The next morning, I noticed that she had sent me a new message. Curiosity caused me to open the message up immediately. She told me that, when she awoke, she noticed that something felt different in her mouth. She explained, "I moved my teeth and tongue around, and I found that everything fits together exactly as it should! I am so amazed! I had an extreme overbite before, but God gave me a miracle in my mouth. It all lines up perfectly." I could feel her excitement as she continued to share with me what God had done. She explained, "The reason that my enamel had worn away was because of the extreme overbite. This overbite caused me to grind my teeth at night. The enamel was worn away because of my teeth grinding."

I didn't know that the cause of her pain was an extreme overbite, but God did. Overnight, He gave her a creative miracle. He went to the cause of the pain and brought complete healing. It is encouraging to know that God is bigger and more powerful than our limited knowledge. As we do our part, He does His.

I'm Confused!

One wintry morning, I opened Facebook and saw a message from a woman who I later learned lives in Africa. She explained in her message that she had fibroids in her uterus and was in extreme pain. Her abdominal area was also enlarged from the fibroids, and her doctor told her that she needed to have surgery to remove her uterus. Because she'd had three surgeries on her uterus already, she did not want to have another one. The previous ones had left her in pain, and she was desperate to be healed. She asked, "Will you pray for me?"

I made arrangements to "meet" her on Facebook chat for prayer later that day. I believe that healing manifests the easiest when a person is receiving the prayer by faith. For that reason, I rarely agree to intercede for a person's healing, but instead I attempt to pray for a person in a more direct way.

We met at the arranged time, and I reminded her that healing already belonged to her because of what Jesus had done at the whipping post. Then I commanded the fibroids to leave her uterus.

"How are you feeling?" I asked.

She answered, "I feel heat in the area where the fibroids are located. Wait! Now I feel cold in that spot. The pain is going! Wow! I don't feel any more pain, but ... I'm confused!"

I was puzzled at that point and asked, "Why are you confused?"

She replied, "I'm letting out gas from my mouth!" I smiled to myself at the humor of it. I knew that she was probably experiencing deliverance. What an unusual way to explain what was happening to her.

I have often seen deliverance happen spontaneously as I have ministered healing to a person. There are several reasons why this may occur. For one reason, the presence of God may cause the demon to manifest. Another reason is that many sicknesses are caused by demons.

I was aware that female health issues are occasionally caused by a particular demon. I also knew that women who deal with this demon often experience dreams about being raped. For this reason, I asked her if she had ever dreamt of being raped in her sleep.

The answer she gave me was both amazing and heartbreaking. She said, "Yes. I was pregnant at the time. I had a dream of being raped, and right after that I lost my baby." Even though it is possible that the dream occurring so close to the loss of the baby was a coincidence, I knew that, in this case, it was not.

I cooperated with what the Holy Spirit was already doing and commanded any remaining demons to get out of her. Then I asked, "How do you feel now?"

She answered, "GREAT! I have no pain left. There is no more 'gas' leaving my mouth, either."

"How is the bloating in your abdomen now?" I asked.

She answered, "It's gone! My stomach is totally flat!" I didn't hear from her again for several more weeks.

I had forgotten all about her remarkable story until I received another message from her on Facebook. She wrote, "You won't believe what happened. I went to my doctor and had another scan. All of the fibroids except for one have disappeared. I don't have to have surgery now." She further explained that, not long after that, the nonstop bleeding had ceased. Because God finishes what He starts, I believe that the last fibroid is gone as well.

Then she told me that she had another request. She said, "I have a painful lump near my navel."

I asked, "Do you know what it is?"

She answered, "No, I have not been to a doctor."

I confidently said, "If God would remove the fibroids, then certainly He would also remove this lump." I commanded, "Lump, whatever you are, get out of her body in the name of Jesus."

She typed, "I think it's shrinking. It is shrinking. It is getting smaller and smaller." By the time I was done praying, the lump was completely gone.

Several weeks later, she sent me a final message. She still had no pain, no excess bleeding, and no lump in her naval area. What a great God!

Happy Tears

Over the years, I have been privileged to pray for many pregnant women with special needs, and I have seen many of them healed. One morning, I received an urgent message from one of these pregnant women. She pleaded, "Please pray for me. I am two months pregnant, and I just found out that I have a blood disorder."

The woman was obviously distraught as she shared with me the details. She explained, "The blood disorder is called thalassemia, and it is characterized by less hemoglobin and fewer red blood cells than normal. The disorder causes severe fatigue and dizziness to those who suffer with it."

Several weeks before she had discovered that she had thalassemia, I had prayed for her because she was experiencing dizziness. The dizziness immediately left, but she did not know that the underlying cause of the dizziness was still there.

I shared with her the simple truth that Jesus healed everyone when He was on Earth, and that He is the same today as He was then. Then I typed a prayer commanding the thalassemia to go from her. I commanded her body to produce the correct level of hemoglobin and red blood cells. I spoke to her body to be healed at a cellular level.

Then I said to her, "Nothing needs to be happening right now in order for you to be healed, but I need to ask you if there is anything happening in case."

She answered, "I'm crying."

I was puzzled and asked, "Why are you crying? Are you crying because you have a blood disorder?"

She answered, saying, "No, no! I am crying because I know that I'm healed. God healed me. I know it. I just know it." I knew that she was crying happy tears, even though I could not see her. What precious, beautiful faith this woman had.

I didn't hear from her for several weeks and had forgotten about our prayer. When she wrote back to me, she had wonderful news. Several weeks later, her husband was tested in order to see if he had thalassemia. Consequently, the doctor decided to perform another blood test with the pregnant mother at the same time.

She wrote, "The doctor called and said that I no longer have the blood disorder. It just isn't there anymore."

Because I wanted to make sure that I had the details of this miracle correct, I asked, "You mean that you had thalassemia the last time they did a blood test, correct?"

She answered, "Yes."

Then I asked, "They did a new blood test and now it is gone, correct?"

Again, she answered, "Yes."

I think that I was more excited than she was. She had been totally convinced that God had healed her, and she expected this good news. There is nothing too hard for our God!

Wrestling with God

One of the difficult things about praying for someone on Facebook chat is that you can't see what they are doing. One Wednesday night, I prayed for a pastor on chat not knowing that he was watching television at the same time.

As I often did, I posted an invitation on my status to meet me in chat for prayer for any physical needs that a person may have. I shared on the same status how I had prayed for someone's knee that day and it had been healed. A woman saw the post and thought of her husband's knee and wrote, "My husband's knee needs healed."

I asked her to call her husband to the computer so that I could pray for him. She called him over to where she was at the computer and explained the situation. He agreed to receive prayer. I didn't realize how little interest he had in receiving prayer though.

He put his hand on his right knee where the pain was as his wife also laid her hand on the knee. I prayed, "Lord, bring complete healing to this knee and drive out all the pain." Then I asked, "How does your knee feel now?"

He answered, "A little better."

I told him, "Wonderful! Let's pray again."

I commanded, "Knee, be healed, and, all pain, go in Jesus' name." After a few more commands, I asked him again, "How does it feel now?" He did not respond. I felt slightly confused because I did not hear from him again, but I quickly forgot about him when others began to ask me for prayer.

On Sunday morning, I found that the pastor had sent my husband an email, and I opened it with a great deal of curiosity. In the email was the rest of the story.

He explained that while I was praying for him he was craning his head around, trying to see what was on television. Of course, I had no idea that he was doing this and continued to pray. To him, the prayer went on and on and on. In fact, he was thinking, *I wish she would stop. My knee hurts and my back hurts from standing this way. I don't want to miss this television show.* What a sense of humor the Lord has. He was at work right in the middle of this humorous situation. The pastor had no idea what the Lord was about to do.

Then he explained in his email that when I was done praying, he stood straight up, and, as he did, he heard the knee pop about a half a dozen times. The popping went right down his knee to where the pain was the worst. He told me us that his knee had never popped like that before. When the popping stopped, the pain was gone. He stood there too shocked to answer my questions on Facebook chat. He just stood there.

He then explained to me how he had hurt his knee. About ten years before, he had begun to work on a friend's vegetable farm. The strain of bending down caught up with him, and, after a time, he began to wear a Velcro brace on his knee. Several months later, he borrowed an elastic knee brace to wear for more support. He wore it for several hours while working on a corn picker, and when he got off of the corn picker, he found that he could not walk. The circulation had been cut off, and the knee had stiffened. His knee was swollen to three times its normal size. After that, all he could do was limp. He limped every day after that until the night I prayed for him, and God healed him.

He continued to explain to me that he had surgery a year later to remove arthritis that had formed in his knee and to smooth out two bone spurs. The surgery was not a success. He had the same pain with the same intensity. He added that he would be paying that medical bill for about ten more years.

He wrote, "I had been prayed for dozens of times and anointed with oil. I had tried ice, rubs, supplements, and medications. I felt like I had wrestled with God, and He had won. I believed that I would limp for the rest of my life. But I have not limped since you prayed for me." He certainly had wrestled with God, and God had won. God's definition of victory is salvation, healing, and deliverance. God had healed him.

As it was a Wednesday night when I prayed for him, the pastor would normally have been at church teaching Bible study, but the service was cancelled because of heavy snow. This was truly a divine appointment.

His wife works at a popular resort in the area where he lives. Her husband often comes to the resort to see her. It was not long before the people who live in his town and those who work at the resort all knew that God had healed him. It could not be hidden because he no longer walked with a limp. The change was obvious. This opened the door for both the pastor and his wife to share God's power and love with many people.

I don't know why the man was healed when I prayed for him and was not healed when others prayed for him. The fact that he eventually was healed is cause for hope though. Never give up on believing God for your healing. Decide that you will believe that He is your Healer no matter how long it takes. He is a faithful and good Father.

"Of Whom the World Was Not Worthy"

There are people who have paid a price to walk with God that most of us know nothing about. This is the testimony of one of them. I have concealed some of the details in order to protect her.

It all started one evening when I received a message in my Facebook inbox from a woman asking for prayer. The woman wrote, "Something happened to me, and now I don't feel so good." I felt deep compassion for her, and we arranged a time to connect for prayer.

When she was online at the arranged time, I asked her how I could pray for her more specifically. After a long wait, she answered, "I can't tell you, but I am in pain all over my body." It was obvious that she did not want me to know what had happened.

I explained to her that Jesus healed everyone who came to Him, so I would expect Him to heal her as well. Then I commanded the pain to go in Jesus' name. It is important after you pray to ask the person what is happening. This enables a person to cooperate with what the Holy Spirit is doing. I asked, "Are you feeling anything that you were not feeling before we prayed? It could be heat or tingling."

She answered, "Something is happening, but I don't know what. I feel 'prickles' all over my body."

"That is the healing power of God," I said with excitement. I knew that she had her miracle.

Then I heard the Lord whisper, "Command the scars to disappear." She had not told me that she had scars, and I had no way of knowing about them with my natural understanding. Father God wanted to demonstrate His care for her in a way that she had never known was possible.

I spoke to the scars to go in Jesus' name several times. Afterwards, she said, "This is crazy! The pain is just about gone, and the bruises are even disappearing." The bruises were leaving right before her eyes.

I felt tenderness towards this precious woman who I knew came from God. He wanted her to know how deeply He cared for her. I went to sleep that night praying for her.

The next day, I noticed that she had sent me another message. I eagerly opened it and read her message with tears in my eyes. She wrote, "This is crazy, but it's a good crazy. I have no pain. In fact, I feel better than I have in a long time. The bruises are gone, and the scars are even disappearing. Some of the scars are totally gone, and some are so light that I can barely see them." Her amazement was evident in her words. She explained to me that she did not like people to see that she had scars on her body because it was embarrassing to her. At a later date, she told me that every scar was completely gone.

Then she asked me, "How did you know about the scars?"

I explained, "It was a word of knowledge. God told me about the scars."

Words of knowledge are a reminder that God sees and cares about every detail of our lives. The next thing she said was so precious that I will never forget it. She said, "I guess God really does like me."

Here is the rest of the story. This woman had been beaten because of her faith in Jesus. She had refused to do something that would have been wrong, and she had been punished for it. It is the sad truth that some people suffer for following God. The writer of Hebrews calls ones such as these "those of whom the world was not worthy." (Hebrews 11:38) Father God will more than compensate them for all that they have suffered one day.

The Lord went beyond healing the pain. He also wanted to erase the reminder of past abuse—the scars themselves. She continued to say, "I guess God really does like me." Indeed, He does.

You May Go Home

Many times, I receive messages on Facebook from someone who is in the hospital. On one of those occasions, a woman wrote to me from her hospital bed and explained that she was in severe pain in the area of her ovary. A CT scan had shown that her ovary was greatly enlarged, and her doctor was concerned that there was a large cyst inside of the enlarged ovary. She told me that a friend had advised her to contact me for prayer.

As I chatted with her through messages, she wrote, "I have a heavy heart because this ovary may have to be removed. You see, just a year ago, my other ovary had to be removed because of a large cyst. I really desire to have children, but I need my ovary."

Then, with great compassion, I began to pray. I said, "Lord, touch her ovary right now. In Jesus' name, anything that should not be in her ovary get out. Ovary, shrink to the correct size, and all pain lift."

As I prayed for her, she said, "My ovary is feeling so hot. Wow! The pain is gone now. It is really gone."

Even though she no longer had pain, she was still nervous

about the ovary. The next day, she was scheduled to have an ultrasound. The ultrasound would show the inside of the ovary and reveal any cysts that were present. She continued to feel anxious while she was having the test done.

After the ultrasound, she waited nervously to find out the results of the test. The doctor entered her room and announced, "I'm not sure what happened, but your ovary is now exactly the right size. There is no cyst and everything is normal. There is no need to stay in the hospital. You may go home."

She walked out of that hospital feeling elated. Our great God had healed her.

Six Hundred Pounds versus God

One evening, as I was praying for people over Facebook chat, I received a message on Facebook from a woman who said, "Would you please pray for my back? I am in so much pain. Ouch! I have had this pain for more than thirty years."

I agreed to pray for her and began to focus on Jesus as her Healer. I thought about how much He loved her and wanted her well. I then reminded her that Jesus healed all who came to Him. I asked the Holy Spirit to touch this woman, and then I commanded the pain to leave her back.

Sometimes it takes more than one prayer or command to see a person healed, but this was not one of those times. After one command, she wrote back, "I feel heat! Wow! The pain is gone! IT'S GONE!" I sensed her joy even though I could not see her face. Thirty years is a long time to be in pain. She had come to Jesus as her Healer, and He had set her free.

For several weeks after that, she often wrote on my Facebook statuses, "My back is still fixed!" She was obviously ecstatic to be without pain. I became curious and decided to ask her what had been wrong with her back.

The story she told me was intriguing. More than thirty years before, she had been a mechanic for an airline. As she was working on a plane one day, a six hundred pound engine fell on her back. The results of that event were several destroyed discs in her spine, nerve damage in her back, and more than thirty years of severe pain. There was nothing that earthly doctors could do to help but, in one moment, the Lord removed every trace of pain.

Do not allow the length of time that you have been sick or in pain stop you from believing for your healing. Nothing is too hard for the Lord. Continue to look to Him as your Healer. Picture yourself in the multitudes coming to Jesus for healing just as they did when He was on Earth. See His compassion for you. Reach out and touch Him as He is reaching out to touch you.

These Things Don't Just Disappear

Very few diagnoses are more feared than that of cancer. The thought of a biopsy causes much stress to those who need it. It is good to know that Jesus is more powerful than even that disease.

A woman contacted me through a healing chat program called "Faith for Healing in Jesus' Name" one evening. She said, "I'm scheduled for biopsy of my uterus. The doctors suspect cancer. I also have numerous cysts and cyst clusters in my uterus, and the doctor says that they appear to be malignant. I had an earlier test that showed cancer bacteria in my uterus, as well. I am so afraid!" I could understand her fear. My heart beat a little faster as I thought of the possibility that she may have cancer, but I turned my heart and mind to the Healer, Jesus Christ.

I reminded her that Jesus had great compassion for her and desired to heal her, and then I began to pray for her. When a person is fearful and highly stressed, I often begin praying for them by commanding the stress to go and then releasing God's presence and peace to them. She quickly felt every muscle in her body relax as God enveloped her with His peace and love. Then, I commanded the cysts, cyst clusters, and cancer bacteria to go from her uterus.

I asked, "Is anything happening right now that you can tell?"

She answered, "I feel tingling in my uterus. It is like chills are going through every cell of my body." God was touching her with His power.

Several weeks later, she contacted me again and left a very different message than her first message. This time, she was filled with joy. She told me that she had had the biopsy, and the doctor had called her to come to his office to discuss the results. He walked into the room where she was waiting and said, "The cysts, the cyst clusters, and the cancer bacteria are all gone." He added, "These things don't just disappear." I would have loved to have seen her face. Even more, I would love to have seen the doctor's face.

The woman told her puzzled doctor, "With prayer they disappear. I received prayer, and Jesus healed me." I don't know how the doctor responded but, again, I would have loved to have seen his face. She went on and on saying, "God is so good. I am so thankful!"

She walked out of the doctor's office with a clean bill of health. Jesus still does miracles today. He is the answer to everything from the common cold to the diagnosis of cancer.

Here Today, Gone Tomorrow

I probably receive more requests for prayer for dental miracles than for anything else. Dental work is expensive where I live, but it may be very difficult, or impossible, to obtain in some other countries.

A woman sent me a message through Facebook messages on one occasion explaining to me that her wisdom tooth had partially broken off. She was in much pain, and she knew that there was a small cavity still in the wisdom tooth. When she tried to eat or to worship, the pain became severe. This situation was complicated by the fact that she lived in an area in Mexico where there was much violence. To get to a dentist, she would have to travel through this turbulent and dangerous area, and she was not able to do that safely. She was desperate for a breakthrough.

I typed a simple prayer as I prayed it aloud. I don't remember the exact words that I used, but I am sure that I would not have even imagined how the Lord planned to take care of this situation.

Several days later, I received another message from her. As I read it, I got so excited that I began to laugh to myself. She explained, "When I woke up the next morning after you prayed for me, I ran my tongue around the back of my mouth to feel the broken off wisdom tooth. You won't believe this, but the tooth was gone!"

I asked her, "Was it possible that the tooth fell out when you slept?"

She answered, "I didn't find it anywhere, and there were no ragged edges and no hole to indicate that it was ever there. There was perfectly smooth skin where the tooth had been."

I wanted to be sure that I understood her, so I asked, "Do you mean it was as if it were never there?"

She answered, "Yes!"

I cannot explain how God performed that miracle, but our God can remove things without leaving any trace of their former presence.

I simply wrote back to her saying, "Jesus was your dentist this week! Praise God!"

The Good Little Jewish Girl

We are often a part of a chain of events in a person's life that God Himself has orchestrated. Paul spoke of people as being like a field that the Lord was cultivating. God's ministers are those that are working in the field. Paul said it well when he said, "I have planted, Apollos watered, but God gave the increase." (I Cor. 3:6)

One evening, as I was praying for people on Facebook chat, I found myself in the midst of God's glorious work in a woman's life. I had posted on my status that I was available to pray for those who were sick or in pain. A beautiful, young woman sent me a message saying, "I am having chest pains, and I can barely breathe. Please pray for me." It didn't take long for me to realize that she was dealing primarily with stress.

As I looked on her Facebook wall, I saw that she was an actress and a writer. I felt as if the Lord had allowed me the privilege of touching a person's life that I could not touch in any other way. *What an honor,* I thought.

I commanded all the stress to leave her body, for the symptoms to stop, and then for the peace of God to fill her. The results were quick and dramatic. She told me, "It all lifted. I feel so much peace. Wow!" As usual, my face lit up with a big smile.

I knew that if she were going to stay in peace, she needed to know the Prince of Peace, so I asked her about her relationship with God. She told me a story that filled me with deep wonder at the faithfulness of our God.

She said, "I grew up as a good little Jewish girl, but my life was interrupted when Jesus visited me in a vision when I was very young. He revealed Himself to me, and I knew then that Jesus was the Messiah. I also knew that I didn't dare tell my parents about what happened, so I just pretended that it didn't." She told me that she decided to continue being a "good little Jewish girl" and forget about the visitation from Jesus. That was her plan, but God had another plan.

She grew up with a desire to act and write. It wasn't long before others noticed her talent, and she began her career. She eventually moved to New York City, the City That Never Sleeps. As she was walking about the city late one night, a man approached her and shared the good news about Jesus with her. All the memories of her visitation with Him as a little girl came flooding back. With deep sincerity, she gave her life to Him.

However, she again walked away from her relationship with Jesus. In spite of this, He never walked away from her. The Lord caused her to see my post stating that I was praying for people on Facebook chat at just the time that she was having the chest pains. She didn't know that God had His hand on her, and this would be the next link in a chain of events that would bring transformation to her life.

After she told me her story, I excitedly said, "God set this encounter up. It was not an accident that you saw my post. He loves you so much, and He desires that you stay free." Then, I added, "Would you like to recommit your life to Him?"

She answered, "YES, from the bottom of my heart!" She joyfully prayed with me, giving her life to God in a fresh way.

Since that time, she has been a witness to artists, writers, and actors in the United States, as well as in other areas of the world. She has reached people that I could not reach. In addition, she never had the chest pains and breathing issues again. I am still in contact with this beautiful, born-again Jewish woman. Her life is not perfect, but she now knows the One who will never leave her or forsake her.

Remember that the Lord knows how to bring every person into a relationship with Him. You may plant the seed or water the seed, but God is faithful to bring the increase.

Laughter Is Good Medicine

There are times when I wish that I could physically see a person while I am praying for them on Facebook chat. I would love to see the dancing eyes and surprised expressions. I would love to hear the amazed voices.

On one of those occasions, a man contacted me on Facebook and wrote, "I am having so much stomach pain. I'm also all bloated. I'm trying not to be afraid, but it isn't working. I'm really nervous about what is wrong with me. Will you pray for me?" I knew that this man had been through some emotional trauma in the last few years, and he was paying the price with physical pain. There were times when I deeply felt the grief in his heart.

I prayed a simple prayer and asked God to drive out the sadness and give him peace. Then I prayed for his healing. He typed, "I don't know what is happening, but I can't stop laughing!" He repeated, "I don't understand this. I just can't stop laughing!" This was when I would have loved to have seen and heard him. He was experiencing the joy of the Lord that was setting him free.

Within a few minutes, he said, "All the pain is gone! Wow! My stomach is back down to its normal size. I'm still laughing!"

His peace and joy were restored as God touched him.

God knows how to bring healing when we don't. When we trust Him and allow Him freedom to touch people the way that He wants to touch them, He can restore people both physically and emotionally.

The joy of the Lord can bring freedom from depression and anxiety, and in this case, it also brought physical healing. "A cheerful heart is good medicine." (Prov. 17:22)

Jumping for Joy

I love it when I get a word of knowledge for healing. When I receive one, the results are often dramatic. I love them so much that I often ask God for more of them.

One night, I heard the Lord tell me that He wanted to heal a vein issue for someone on Facebook. I usually recognize a word of knowledge such as this by an "inner knowing". I posted on my status a call for anyone needing healing in their veins to meet me in Facebook chat. *This is going to be fun!* I thought.

It didn't take long for a woman to send me a message saying, "I have varicose veins that are so painful I can't get anything done. My house is a mess." Faith rose in her heart as she realized that God cared about the pain she was going through. He picked her out of all those who would be reading my post that night.

I reminded her that Jesus paid for her healing already. Then I typed, "Lord, cause Your power to go through her veins right now. Varicose veins, untwist. Veins, be completely healed. Pain, leave her legs. Swelling, go down."

As I prayed, she said, "I feel heat in my legs and ankles." Then she exclaimed, "The deep purple color is disappearing, and the veins are becoming a light color! Wow! The swelling is all going down as well, and the pain is all gone!"

Right in front of her eyes, she saw a miracle unfold. She decided to put the miracle to the test and began to jump up and down vigorously. She stopped and thought, *I'll try that again.* She again began to jump up and down. Still there was no pain. No matter how hard she jumped, she had no symptoms of the varicose veins. I would have loved to have been a mouse in her living room.

Jesus paid a high price for our physical healing at the whipping post. He also paid for things that are even deeper in our hearts. This woman had been through much trauma in her life because of a cancer that she had experienced. God saw the deeper need inside of her, and He touched that need in a beautiful way. She said, "I can't stop laughing. The joy of the Lord is consuming me!" Oh, how she needed that.

She sent me a message several days later saying, "I still have no pain, no swelling, and no deep purple color in my veins. I'm completely healed and have been able to catch up with my housework. God is awesome!"

Voodoo

Much of my on-the-job training in healing took place on Facebook. I have encountered a multitude of different diseases and people this way. Because the nations meet on Facebook, I often encountered situations that were unfamiliar to me. This situation was extremely unfamiliar.

I received a message one morning in my Facebook inbox from a woman who wrote, "I need prayer. I'm waking up with burn marks on my body. I also have stomach pain."

I felt puzzled and asked, "Do you know how the burn marks are getting there?"

She answered, "No, I have no idea. They are just appearing."

Then I heard a word in my spirit. The word was "voodoo".

I asked, "Is it possible that you have been a victim of voodoo?"

She answered, "Yes. I have relatives who practice voodoo. One family member who practices voodoo is very upset with me because of my relationship with God." I took a quick glance at her Facebook wall and realized that she lived in a nation in which voodoo is common.

I had never ministered to anyone who had been a victim of voodoo before, but I simply leaned on God's power. He knows what to do when I don't. I commanded, "Every unclean, tormenting spirit that is causing these burn marks, go from her now in the name of Jesus. She is free because of the blood of Jesus." Then I added, "Lord, drive out the stomach pain as well."

I waited a few moments, and then I asked her how she felt. She replied, "The pain in my stomach is completely gone."

I wrote back, "That is wonderful! Praise God! I will continue to believe that you will never again wake up with burn marks on your body." As I normally do, I forgot about her situation.

Several days later, I noticed a new message in my Facebook inbox from this woman. She wrote, "I have not woken up with any burn marks since you prayed for me. Besides that, the scars on one side of my body have totally disappeared! I can barely see the scars on the other side of my body. Praise God!" *What an awesome God!* I thought. I wanted to shout His greatness from the rooftops. Even though I did not hear from her again, I am sure that the last traces of the scars completely disappeared, as well.

It is easy for God to remove scars. There is nothing too hard for Him. The name of Jesus is greater than any defeated demon. The name of Jesus is greater than voodoo.

When you minister healing to many people, you will encounter situations that are unfamiliar. It is important to listen to the Holy Spirit, but if you do not hear specific directions, remember that God knows how to resolve the issue. Trust Him to do what you don't know how to do. He knows it all.

Supernatural Expansion

One evening, a woman contacted me on Facebook messages and asked, "Would you pray for me? I had breast cancer last year, and I want you to pray that any stray cancer cells will disappear." She did not know it, but she was going to receive much more than that.

I reminded myself and the woman of God's promises of healing. Then I commanded, "Any stray cancer cells, get out of her body in the name of Jesus." Then I asked her if anything unusual was happening.

She replied, "I feel heat in my arm. Wow! I can lift my arm. This morning I could not even move it. I haven't been able to brush my own hair in weeks." In a few minutes, she added, "The pain and swelling in my arm is totally gone as well. I couldn't touch it without excruciating pain before you prayed. Wow!"

Since she had not asked for prayer for her arm, I was confused. Curiously, I asked, "What was wrong with your arm?" I knew that God had gone beyond what I knew to ask Him to do.

She said, "I had lymphedema." I had a little bit of understanding of lymphedema, but I was curious enough that I searched online to find out more about it. I read that, because lymph nodes had been removed, her lymph system had become damaged. The lymph vessels could no longer adequately drain lymph fluid because of the damage. The result had been pain and swelling, but God removed it all. How gracious God is! He went beyond what I had asked.

The woman's miracle gets even more exciting than that. She was in the process of having breast reconstruction done. In the procedure that she was to have, a short-term tissue expander was inserted. The expander is a balloon-like sac that is slowly expanded over a period of two to three months. On a regular basis, the surgeon would insert a saltwater solution. This would continue until the skin was stretched adequately to support breast reconstruction.

She explained, "Having the saltwater solution inserted is so painful. The stretching really hurts. Would you pray that the skin and the expander will expand without any more treatments or insertion of saltwater solutions?" She asked me to pray for a creative miracle.

When I heard her request, I was quite aware that she was a woman of great faith. Perhaps her faith was enlarged when God healed the lymphedema.

"In Jesus' name, I command the expander to expand all on its own. Lord, give her this miracle," I prayed. I also spoke to the pain that she had from her last treatment to leave her body. Instantly, the pain disappeared.

I heard from her about a week later. She wrote, "I just got back from my surgeon, and God gave me my miracle. He measured my breast as he always did, but when he measured it this time, it was just the right size."

I wanted a clarification of what had happened, so I asked, "Does that mean that the expander expanded all on its own?"

She answered, "Yes, it expanded all on its own. My surgeon told me that I did not need to have anymore insertions."

She got her miracle because she asked and because she dared to believe. God's mercy and grace is abundant. Do not hesitate to ask for your miracle. Nothing is impossible with Him.

Miracles in the Marketplace

My Journey - The Threefold Cord of Healing

A number of years ago, I began to desperately cry out to the Lord to teach me how to grow in the area of healing. At first, God did not seem to answer me, but then, one day, as I was driving and praying for wisdom, the answer came. The Lord brought a Scripture to my mind found in Ecclesiastes 4:12. "A threefold cord is not easily broken."

I knew that the Lord was showing me that if I would bring three things together in my life, they would result in a strong healing ministry. Then I asked the obvious question: "Lord, what are the three strands in this cord?" He quickly spoke three things to me.

The first "strand" that He showed me was the area of the renewing of my mind. The renewing of the mind is needed in order to have strong faith for healing. Anyone who wants to see the sick healed must know that the Lord wants to heal every single person standing in front of them. Jesus healed all who came to Him, and He is the same today as He was when He was on Earth. He did not refuse to heal any person for any reason. Jesus is the perfect picture of the will of God.

It is equally true that anyone who wants to see the sick healed must believe that God will heal through them. The Bible tells us that believers shall lay hands on the sick, and they shall recover. (Matthew 16:18) The only qualification is to be a believer. Some mistakenly think that you must have a gift of healing in order to see the sick healed, but this is not correct. Neither is it true that you must walk in a particular spiritual office. If you are a believer, you can heal the sick.

I spent many hours reading Matthew, Mark, Luke, and John over and over and over again. This time spent in the Word caused me to develop a strong faith in God's desire and power to heal every person I saw.

The second "strand" that the Lord revealed to me was in the area of relationship with the Holy Spirit. This is the area of encounters, impartation, and intimacy with the Holy Spirit.

We have all that we need to see the sick healed when we are baptized in the Holy Spirit, but encounters with the Holy Spirit bring a new depth to what we already have. These encounters clear away hindrances in our emotions or mind that prevent the power of God from flowing. They cause bondages of fear, condemnation or wrong motives to be broken. Through these encounters, the Lord imparts internal strength to enable us to meet the demands that may come as we minister. Paul said that he longed to see the Romans so that he could impart some spiritual gift. (Romans 1:11) He told Timothy to stir up the gift that was in him through the laying on of hands. (II Timothy 1:6)

Several years ago, I had a series of encounters with the Holy Spirit in which I was stuck to the ground for hours in His presence. During one of these encounters, the evangelist left me in the hotel meeting room under the power of God. After a while, my back started to hurt from being unable to move on the hard floor. As I was lying there, unable to get up, a hotel worker walked in three times, looked at me in confusion, and then walked out. It was embarrassing, but my desire and hunger for God was stronger than any embarrassment I faced. I noticed a great increase in miracles after those encounters. Tumors started disappearing at an increased rate. The presence of God rested on my words and ministry in a greater way.

In addition to the encounters that the Lord gives us, it is important to learn to flow with the Holy Spirit in ministry. The Lord taught me that my focus must always rest on the Holy Spirit inside of me. If I were to turn my attention to myself or my successes and failures, I would disconnect from the power source. The power source is the Holy Spirit living inside of the believer. That power is accessed through faith in Jesus and focus on His presence.

The last "strand" that the Lord showed me was faithfulness. If you want much you must be faithful in little. That which we use will grow. Faithfulness causes you to refuse to quit no matter what difficulties may arise. There are times when ministering in healing is difficult. That is the time to dig in your heels and continue to be faithful.

These three "strands"—renewing of the mind, intimacy with the Holy Spirit, and faithfulness—are all essential to grow in healing ministry. They are the intertwining of body, soul, and spirit. With our soul or mind, we learn to think correctly. With our spirit, we connect with the Holy Spirit, our power source. Finally, with our body, we develop faithfulness—the ability to persevere.

The Shaking Man

For a period of time in my life, I would go to a local soup kitchen to pray and minister to people on a weekly basis. Sometimes my heart would break as I saw them come into this dark, dreary room to get a meal with their families. The food, although adequate, was not especially nutritious. They often ate in silence, and many had little joy in their hearts.

On one of those days at the soup kitchen, I walked in and saw a man sitting by himself, desperately trying to get the spoon to his mouth. Every move he made was accompanied by jerking motions. He was slowly able to feed himself. I felt such deep compassion for him. I went over, sat across from him, and asked, "May I pray for you when you are done eating?"

He gratefully answered, "I-I-I would a-a-a-ppreciate that." He struggled to get every word out because his voice was shaking so much.

I inquired, "What's wrong?"

He answered, "I have a neurological disease." He told me the name of the disease, but I had never heard of it before. Not wanting to embarrass him, I went and sat at another table until he was done eating.

As he got up from the table, I noticed that he was also walking with a slow, jerky gait. I directed him to a small chapel that was adjacent to the soup kitchen so that I could pray for him. I shared with him why Jesus would heal him, laid a hand on his shoulder, and began to ask God to touch him. All the while, he was shaking and jerking under my hand.

I prayed, "Lord, drive this all out. In Jesus' name, I command this disease to go from him." Right under my hand, all the shaking stopped. A look of total peace settled on him. It was beautiful and amazing to see the healing power of our God.

He looked at me with huge eyes and said, "I felt electricity go all through my body!" Then, with a now completely clear voice, this man cried out, "Lord, forgive me. I'm sorry. I have been so far from You. I give my life to You." Without a word from me, he called on the name of the Lord for salvation.

As he walked away from me that day, the jerking and the shaking were gone. More than that, he walked out from there as a brand new creation in Christ.

Any form of evangelism that brings forth fruit is good, but God has a "master plan" for evangelism. He instructed his disciples to both proclaim the good news and to heal the sick. (Luke 10:9) In this case, the Lord drew this man through a miracle without a word from me. The Lord intended that every one of His disciples continue on with the "master plan". One life changed is well worth any challenge that may be encountered.

Sammy

It is amazing the treasure that you will find in people if you go looking for it. Each person is precious to the Lord regardless of their current condition. I found such a treasure one day in a young man who I now know is named Sammy.

As I was driving through town, I saw Sammy sitting on a bench in a small park and I decided that I would offer to pray for him. I parked my car across from the park where he was seated, and I locked my door. As I walked across the road, I felt the strangest sensation. I sensed anger and hatred pouring out from him. Even though I was not close to him, I seemed to be able to feel what was inside of his heart.

A sudden rush of thoughts hit me. *What if he steals my purse? I forgot to lock it in the trunk. What if he has a knife?* For the first time that I could remember, I felt fear in approaching a person on the street.

It is wise to listen to the Holy Spirit in moments like that, but I knew that this fear was not from Him. I determined not to allow fear to stop me. I picked up my stride toward where he was sitting.

As I walked up to him, I noticed that his eyes were dark and clouded. His face reflected the anger that was in his heart. I clutched my purse close to me and asked, "Is there any way that I can pray for you today?"

Sammy never looked up at me but I could still see his dark, angry eyes. He spoke with a desperate tone in his voice. "Yeah, you can pray for me. I want to be a better person. I have so much anger and hatred." *That is no surprise to me*, I thought.

I felt deep compassion for him, and I said, "I know a way that you can be a brand new person inside. Do you want that?"

He said, "Yes, I do."

I replied, "Pray this with me. I want you to repeat what I say, but speak it to God."

Normally, I would share the simple gospel in a situation like this, but in that moment it didn't seem to be necessary. I led him in a prayer in which he asked God to forgive him. He repeated a sincere cry to God to make him a new person and to come and live inside of him.

What happened next was astounding. Sammy stood up, looked right into my eyes with a huge smile on his face, and then he gave me a warm hug. There was no hatred in his eyes any longer, and I felt the love of God emanating from him.

I began to share with Sammy in more detail what God had just done for him, and I encouraged him to continue walking with God. He already had a Bible, and I referred him to a nearby church. I have seen Sammy many times since then. He still has that bright smile on his face, he still has no anger or hatred in his eyes, and he is still walking with God. When I ask him if he needs prayer, he always says, "No. I'm doing just fine since you prayed with me the last time."

There are people like that everywhere. All they need is a believer to introduce them to Jesus. They are God's treasures waiting to be found.

Jesus' Power Trumps New Age

We live in a world that has embraced power from many sources. There are an estimated 50,000 Wiccans in the United States alone. There are thousands of others, although not Wiccan, who practice Reiki or some other type of energy healing. If we are to reach these people, we must walk in a level of power that is greater than their level of power.

As I was shopping one day, a woman I know walked up to me with her friend. She introduced her friend and then said, "My friend needs healing in her right shoulder. She is in so much pain. She also has ear problems that cause vertigo all the time. I wondered if you would pray for her."

I spoke to both of these ladies about the price Jesus paid on the cross for our healing. Then I told the woman needing healing that I would like to pray for her shoulder first. I asked, "Can you lift your arm up?" The woman slowly tried to lift her arm, but she could not lift it above her shoulder. Her faced reflected her excruciating pain.

I prayed, "Lord, drive that pain out. In Jesus' name, shoulder be healed and well."

She said, "I feel heat." She went on to explain, "I go to a 'healer' who uses crystals to chase away the bad energy. I feel heat then, but I never thought I would feel heat from prayer." She went on to explain to me that when she felt heat, the pain would leave for a while, but it always came back.

Jesus never engaged in healing that involved crystals or energy, and He is our pattern for life and ministry. Neither did the disciples minister healing in this way. When Peter healed a lame man, he explained, "And His name, through faith in His name, has made this man strong…" (Acts 3:16) Jesus paid a terrible price at the whipping post for our healing. I have a zealous desire that He, and He alone, will receive the glory for miracles, not crystals or any other thing. Faith in His name, and the price that He paid, brings healing.

I earnestly prayed in my heart that the Lord would show this woman that His power is much greater than that which could be found in a crystal. When the heat from her shoulder was gone, I said to her, "Raise your arm up." Her arm shot straight up, and her eyes opened wide with shock.

Then I prayed for her ears. Instantly, she told me, "I don't hear the ringing anymore." I didn't know that she had ringing in her ears at all. All I knew about was the vertigo. Then she continued to say, "The vertigo is gone!" She was visibly excited. She explained that the crystals never healed the vertigo or the ringing.

It was my delight to tell her, "You experienced God's power. It is stronger than crystals."

Months later, I found out that the pain in her shoulder and the vertigo and ringing in her ears never returned. She continually talked to her friends about how amazed she was that God had healed her. The best part of all was that her friend was able to share the gospel with this woman. I am confident that I will see her in Heaven someday because of the love and power of God that she experienced in healing.

Jesus trumps New Age practices. The power of Jesus' name is far greater than any other power. We must go to those in the occult with a demonstration of that power. Words alone will not win them. The good news is that we have the source of that power inside of us in the person of the Holy Spirit.

"For our gospel came not unto you in word only, but also in power and in the Holy Ghost..." (I Thess. 1:5)

Kept Alive by a Dream

One morning, as I woke up, I heard the Holy Spirit tell me that He was sending me to someone who needed ministry that day. A few hours later, I drove to a small park to look for the person who I knew was a "treasure" to the Lord. I saw a group of young men playing football, and I sensed the Lord whispering to me, "One of them has pain in his shoulder." I knew that the one with pain was the one He desired to touch.

I walked up to the group and loudly asked, "Does anyone here have pain in his shoulder?"

One of the men looked at me and answered with a suspicious tone to his voice, "Ye-e-e-s." The rest of the young men moved a little farther away and continued their football game. The man with the sore shoulder just stared at me.

I explained, "I believe that God told me about your shoulder because He wants to heal you."

The young man relaxed a little and said, "I believe in God. When I was sixteen, something strange happened to me. I became very sick and was in unbearable pain. My organs began to shut down, and the doctors told me that I was dying. They had done test after test, but none of the tests revealed what was wrong with me. You won't believe what happened next!"

That piqued my curiosity, and I asked, "What happened next?"

He continued, "One night, as I lay in that hospital room sleeping, I had a dream. I dreamed that the problem was an infection in my tooth. When I woke up, I told the nurses and doctors, they did some tests, and it was an infected tooth. We caught it just in time, and that is why I am alive today."

Now I knew why the Lord had led me to this particular man. God had preserved this young man's life through a dream so that he would come to know Him some day. What a merciful God!

I asked the young man if I could pray for his shoulder, and he allowed me to do that. After several prayers and commands, the pain was gone.

Then I said to him, "God loves you so much. He saved your life through a dream, and now He has sent me to give you a message." I shared with the young man that Jesus is the only way to Heaven. I told him that Jesus had paid the price for his freedom and salvation, and He was waiting with open arms for him to receive His free gift of eternal life. I told him, "Besides that, the Holy Spirit will come and live inside of you. He will make you a brand new person. Are you ready to give your life to God?"

The young man said, "Yes, I am." As the presence of God filled that park, he gave his life to Jesus.

It is all about God's amazing love. He has that same love for every person you will see tomorrow and for the rest of your life. He watches over each person on the earth and woos them into the Kingdom. At times, He may send dreams to reveal Himself to them or even to save their lives. What a privilege we have to co-labor with Him to reach those who He dearly loves.

Out of the Hospital and into God's Healing

One spring day, as I drove into the parking lot of a soup kitchen where I often ministered, I saw a man and a woman walking towards the door. I noticed that the woman had a large bandage on her bulging stomach. *What is wrong with her?* I wondered. I knew this was a setup from the Lord.

I approached the couple and asked the woman, "What happened?" She told me that she had just gotten out of the hospital and was walking over to the soup kitchen to get something to eat. She had been in the hospital because of an infection she had gotten from a metal. The infection had spread all through her body and had caused the bulge in her stomach. Even though the hospital had treated her, the doctors felt that there was little that they could do at that time.

I asked her if she was in pain. She answered, "Horrible pain! They sent me home with a prescription for pain medicine, but I can't afford to buy it. What good is a prescription if you don't have any money?"

I explained, "God can drive out every bit of that pain." I

shared with her a simple illustration that I had learned from a healing minister, Roger Sapp. I said, "If I could put you in a time machine and send you back to when Jesus was on Earth, He would heal you. I know that because He healed everyone. He is the same now as He was then." Then I asked her if I may pray for her. She was more than willing to receive prayer.

As I laid hands on her, I noticed that her eyes widened with surprise, and she said, "I feel tingling in my stomach." In a few moments, she added, "The pain is all gone." I prayed again, and this time she felt tingling go through her entire body. Right in front of our eyes, the bulge underneath the bandage disappeared. She felt around her stomach area and said with wide eyes, "I can't find the bulge!"

The woman began to explain to me that they attended a church. I said, "Great! In your journey towards God, have you come to the place in which you know you will spend eternity with the Lord?"

I noticed a slight look of confusion on both of their faces, and they answered, "No." They added, "We probably would not spend eternity with God." It is amazing how many people do not have that assurance of eternal life.

I explained to them that God had me at just the right place and time to bring them good news. I told them that God loved them and was waiting for them with open arms. If they would put their trust in what Jesus had done when He died on the cross for them and call on His name, He would come and live inside of them. I further explained that God would not force a relationship on them. This was a choice that they would need to make. When I asked them if they wanted to pray with me and receive Jesus as their Savior and Lord, they quickly agreed.

The three of us held hands as I led them in a prayer to the Lord. After we were done praying, I noticed the joy and peace on their faces.

After we had prayed, they went into the soup kitchen to eat. I also went in and prayed with a few people. When the couple was done eating, I noticed them walking towards the door. The woman still had a totally flat stomach, along with a smile on her face.

Mark 16:20 (Amp) says it well: "And they went everywhere, while the Lord kept working with them and confirming the message by the attesting signs and miracles that closely accompanied it."

The Sinner Woman

One of the lies that Satan loves to tell believers is that no one wants to hear the truth of the gospel. However, the Bible tells us a different story. Jesus said that the harvest is great. The real problem is that the laborers are few. (Luke 10:2)

I was walking down a city sidewalk one day when I saw two women sitting on a bench. I wanted to offer to pray for them, but they were so deep in conversation that I decided to walk past them. However, as I was directly beside them, I heard one of the women say, "My neck hurts SO bad. I'm on my way to the hospital to have an x-ray taken of it."

I stopped in my tracks and thought, *Wow! I think God just set me up.*

I spoke to the woman with the painful neck and said, "I am sorry to interrupt you, but I couldn't help hearing you say that your neck hurts. I am a Christian, and the Bible says that believers will lay hands on the sick, and they will recover. May I pray for you?"

She graciously answered, "Yes, you may pray for me." I laid hands on her neck, commanding the pain to go, and then I asked her to check it. She told me, "The pain is gone!"

Just then, a bus came, and she told us, "I have to get on the bus to get to the hospital." She hurried on to the bus with a smile on her face.

Then I turned to the other woman and asked, "How about you? Is there some way that I may pray for you?"

She looked at me sadly and said, "Yes, my husband died two weeks ago, and I miss him so much!"

"Oh, I am so sorry," I told her. I listened as she told me about her beloved husband. Then I took her hand and prayed that the Lord would comfort her with His peace.

I knew that I needed to be gentle, but also bold in how I shared the good news of the gospel with her. As I prayed in my heart for wisdom, I asked, "How about you? Do you know that you would spend eternity with the Lord if you died today?"

Her answer shocked me. She said, "Oh, no. I know I wouldn't spend eternity with God. I am such a sinner!"

I knew now why the Lord had directed me to these women and then made it obvious to me that I should speak to them. This dear woman who had just lost her husband was ready to come to know Jesus.

I joyfully said, "I have wonderful news for you. Jesus took the punishment for every sin that you have ever committed." I continued to explain to her how much God loved her. I told her that He would make her a brand new person inside.

After speaking to her for a few minutes, I asked, "Are you ready to give your life to Jesus?"

She answered, "Oh, yes. I ASK GOD EVERY NIGHT WHAT TO DO ABOUT MY SINS!" My heart melted as I thought of the deep concern and worry that this woman carried. The Lord is so faithful though. He answered her question by sending me. She prayed with me in a deeply sincere voice. Afterwards, her face was full of a newfound peace and joy.

The harvest truly is ripe.

The Man Who Had Died

On a warm, sunny Saturday, I decided to go out for some "fishing". I don't like to fish for fish, but I very much like to fish for souls. As I walked through a nearby downtown area, I noticed a middle-aged man with a cane sitting on a bench. I approached him and asked if he had any pain in his body. He replied, "Oh, yes. I have pain all the time." I felt compassion rise up inside of me for this man.

I explained to him that if I could take him back to when Jesus was on Earth, He would have healed him because Jesus healed everyone who came to Him. I reminded him that Jesus is the same now as He was then. I asked if I could lay my hand on him and pray for him. He gratefully shook his head up and down. After I prayed a simple prayer commanding the pain to go, I asked him how he felt. He told me, "The pain is completely gone!"

Then the man told me how the pain started. He said, "Seven years ago, I was driving a truck down the highway, and I had an accident. The truck flipped over, and I died. In fact, I was dead for ten minutes before they brought me back to life."

I asked, "Do you remember anything from that time when

you were dead?"

He answered, "No, but I am so thankful that they brought me back."

I saw the perfect moment to lower the "bait". I said to him, "I am so glad that the Lord gave you another chance at life. Let me ask you a question. What if you would not have come back to life? Do you know where you would be spending eternity?"

He replied, "No, I guess I don't."

The man listened intently as I explained that Jesus gave His life for him so that he could live. Jesus loved him and wished to forgive every sin and come and live inside of him. I assured him that he would be a new creation when he gave his life to Jesus. When I was finished sharing the simple gospel with him, I asked, "Are you ready to give your life to God and invite Him to be your Lord and Savior?"

He answered with deep conviction in his voice, "Yes, I am." We prayed together, and I went on my way rejoicing.

As I walked away, questions rushed through my mind. What if God brought that man back from the dead because He knew that I would walk past him someday and share Jesus with him? What if I would have stayed home that day in disobedience to the Lord? How many other times has God performed a miracle so that someone would have an opportunity to accept Him?

I contemplated God's great love for the man. He desired that this man would come to know Him, and He allowed me to lead him straight to the heart of the Father.

God has divine appointments for every one of us. Our part is to go. God may bring someone back from the dead because He knows that you will speak to that person someday.

I have seen this man many times since that day. He still has no pain, and he is still walking with Jesus. Someday, I will see him in eternity.

The Transvestite

I was walking down a city sidewalk one day when I saw what appeared to be two men sitting on a bench. I knew that the Lord wanted me to minister to them, and my heart started to beat faster in anticipation of what God would do.

As I got closer, I noticed that one of them had some feminine characteristics. It was obvious that she had purposely dressed in such a way and cut her hair to appear to be a man even though she was a woman. I knew that she was a transvestite, but she was a transvestite that God loved.

When I was right in front of them, I asked if they had pain in their bodies. I explained that I was a Christian and I believed that God heals today. The transvestite said, "My back is killing me!" She spoke in a lowered tone of voice in order to sound like a man.

I replied, "Jesus healed everyone who came to Him, and He is the same now as He was when He was on Earth. May I pray for you?"

The transvestite looked relieved as a glimmer of hope and faith came into her eyes.

Some might wonder if God would heal a transvestite, but the answer to that is found by looking at the life of Jesus. He healed everyone in the multitudes when He was on Earth, and most certainly some of them were living a sinful lifestyle. He loved this transvestite as He loves everyone. God responds to faith for healing whether it is demonstrated by a Christian or a person who is still outside of Christ.

I laid my hand on her back and commanded the pain to go. A look of surprise came into her eyes as she said, "The pain is gone!"

The man who was sitting beside her spoke up and said, "I have pain in my neck. Would you pray for me too?"

"I would be glad to," I said. After I prayed, he checked his neck and found that his pain was also gone. I told both of them, "Jesus paid for your sin and for your healing. He loves you and wants to have a relationship with you. Are you ready to turn from every sin and give Him your life?"

They both answered, "Yes, I am."

Right there, the two people sitting on the bench bowed their heads and asked God to forgive them and to come and live inside of them.

No one is beyond God's love or His reach. When we demonstrate the reality of God's power, lives are changed.

Funny You Should Ask

Years ago, I went through a season in which I was asking the Lord to give me words of knowledge concerning places where He wanted me to minister. I would often ask Him where He wanted me to go. Sometimes I got an answer, and sometimes, I did not. One snowy, wintry day, I again asked Him, "Is there anywhere You want me to go today?" His answer was swift. I felt as if I heard Him tell me to go to the mall.

Although I was greatly lacking in confidence, I quickly got ready and drove about twenty-five miles to the local mall. When I got there, I walked around asking, "God, who is it?" In a short while, I saw a young woman sitting by herself watching TV. I knew that she was the one.

I noticed that she was watching a plane crash on television, so I walked up to her and said, "Scary isn't it?"

She looked at me with fear in her eyes and said, "Yes, I have to fly home from college in a few days."

I realized that this was my opportunity. "May I pray that you will have a safe flight home?"

She quickly answered, "Yes, please do."

I prayed that the Lord would protect her, and then I said, "I know that you are going to make it home safely, but let me ask you a question. If you were to die today or a hundred years from now, do you know for sure that you would spend eternity with the Lord?" By this time, my compassion was stirred for this beautiful, young lady.

Her answer was astounding. She looked at me with the most surprised look on her face and said, "Funny you should ask. My boyfriend and I have been going to different churches looking for the answer to that question."

I was shocked. She had visited many churches and had not gotten an answer to her question. What a sad indictment against the churches that she had visited.

I asked, "What made you even think about where you would spend eternity?"

She answered, "I have been taking a course in Greek mythology in college. In Greek mythology, the 'gods' can throw you in hell for almost anything. My boyfriend and I have been concerned about what the Bible really teaches." God had used a college course to draw her and speak to her.

I knew that God had directed me to the right person. I was filled with a sense of wonder at His goodness. I said, "I have great news for you. I can tell you what the Bible says." I shared the simple good news of how much God loved her and how Jesus gave His life for her. It was only a matter of moments before she was praying with me, giving her life to Him. God saw her hungry heart and sent me to bring in the harvest. His love is so great for each individual on the planet. Amazing!

I referred her to a good church in her area, and went on my way rejoicing. It is a great honor to co-labor with the Holy Spirit to see the lost saved and the sick healed. Listen to His still, small voice, and God will direct you to those whom He is preparing.

I'm Going to Kill Myself Tonight

I woke up one morning with anticipation raging inside of me. I was planning on attending an Aglow outreach at a local park in Erie, PA, and I knew that God had something special planned that day. However, I had no idea what that might have been.

I picked up a friend, and we chatted with each other as I drove to the park. When we arrived, there were quite a few women already there. I spoke to several of them and listened as a worship leader led those in attendance in a time of praise and worship. What happened next during praise and worship became a blur as my mind began to wander. I looked around at the people who were walking through the park and wondered if they knew Jesus. I wondered who needed healed. It wasn't long before I felt as if I could not stand there without speaking to the park visitors for one more moment.

I saw a young man riding his bike through the park, and I felt drawn to him. I didn't hear the Lord tell me to speak to him, but I noticed compassion rising up inside of me for him. The Lord often leads me in this simple way. By this time, I felt as if I couldn't get to him fast enough. As I walked towards him, I prayed that he would not ride away too quickly for me to reach him.

When I was standing beside him, I said, "Excuse me, sir. Do you have any pain in your body today?"

He answered in a slow, labored voice, "No, no pain."

I whispered a prayer in my heart asking God to lead me in what to say to this young man next.

Without thinking, I asked, "Has anyone ever told you that God loves you?"

His jaw dropped open, and he looked at me with big eyes. Tears began to well up, and he said, "I can't believe it! I just can't believe it! This morning, I told God that if someone did not tell me that He loved me, I was going to kill myself tonight."

By that time, I had some tears myself. He continued, "I just couldn't go on without knowing that God still cared about me. I just can't believe this!"

I asked him, "How has your relationship with God been lately?"

He answered sadly, "Pretty nonexistent. I received him as my Savior years ago, but then I got caught up in drugs. I thought that He was mad at me because of that. It felt like I had no hope any longer."

I replied, "Now you know that God has never abandoned you. His love has never been withdrawn from you. The proof is that He sent me to you. Would you like to pray right now with me and recommit your life to Him?"

"I sure would," he said.

He prayed along with me and reaffirmed his relationship to the Lord. I commanded the addiction to drugs to be broken, and then he went on his way a happy man. I watched as he drove his bike away from me, and I marveled at the goodness of God. I was thankful for the privilege of being a part of this young man's miracle.

I'm Not Religious Either

On one hot summer day, I decided to visit a "not too nice" part of town. This is the part of town where drug houses are on every other corner. Because it was daytime, and God was with me, I was not at all afraid.

As I walked down the street, I saw a group of young men and women sitting on a porch. Some of them were sitting in chairs and some were sitting on the steps. I knew that this was a drug house. I sensed God's love for each one of them.

I walked up to them and made some casual conversation. "Sorry to interrupt you. Sure is hot today, isn't it?" They were polite and friendly, but I'm sure they wondered why I was even bothering to talk to them. They were young. I was not so young.

Then I got right to the point. "I'm out today praying for people who need healing. Do any of you have pain in your body?"

One young man spoke up and said, "Uh, we aren't religious."

I answered and said, "Oh, OK. I'm not religious either."

They looked back and forth at each other with confusion.

Nervous laughter echoed through the area. I certainly had their attention.

Not wanting to lose my opportunity, I quickly said, "I don't have 'religion'. I have a relationship." Then I explained, "Religion is when man tries to get to God. My Jesus came to me. No matter how good you or I try to be, we will never be good enough to have a relationship with Him. We would have to be perfect. Because Jesus loved us so much, He came to Earth, gave his life for us, and now He invites us to have a relationship with Him."

They watched me intently. There was not one more giggle or smirk. I felt the presence of God descend on us, and I knew that the Lord was speaking to their hearts.

The prophetic is not my strongest gift, but this time it was the Lord's gift of choice. I turned to one young man and said, "You look like you are tough, but inside you are a teddy bear. In fact, you are the one who is the quickest to protect all of the others. You can't stand to see a person hurt."

The look on his face was priceless. His eyes widened in amazement. He said, "That's true."

His friends then began to laugh. They said, "I can't believe you knew that. How did you know that?"

I explained, "The Lord told me. He wants you to know how real He is and how much He loves you."

The Lord gave me something to share with each person on

the porch that day. Every eye was on me, and they continued to say, "I can't believe you knew that!"

After I was finished speaking to each one of them, I said, "Are you ready to give your lives and hearts to Him?" Each one of them shook their heads and said, "Yes."

I led them in a prayer, and every one of them sincerely repeated the prayer after me. Salvation is a matter of the heart. It does not come from saying the perfect set of words. I saw that heart in them.

I did not see that group of young men and women again, but the Holy Spirit knows how to continue working in their lives. I know that His love for them will never end.

What a wonderful God we have who could take a "not so young" woman to reach the young. How amazing that He would give the "not so prophetic" woman a word of knowledge for each one of them. He longs to reveal Himself to people, and He wants to demonstrate His love to them. It is our privilege to be a part of His amazing grace.

Miracles in Services

My Journey - If You Don't Go…

I had been ministering in the area of healing for several years when I faced a new challenge. I had become comfortable with ministering on the streets, on Facebook, and in my own church, but my heart desired something more. I wanted to have healing services in other churches as well.

Along with this desire came many questions. Is this really God's will? Am I seeing enough people healed to have healing services? Am I ready for such a step as this? The questions and concerns plagued my mind and kept me from moving forward.

Then, one night, I had a dream. In my dream, I was invited to minister at a large church. I arrived a little early and watched the people pour into the room. Suddenly, my mind became flooded with concern. I thought, *I am not ready. I need visuals.* Since I had taught young children at an earlier time in my life that thought seemed natural in my dream. I rushed off to find "visuals".

After I found what I was looking for, I headed back to the church. As I entered the room, I was shocked to see a man in the front of the church pelting out a patriotic song to the crowd of people. Then the man said, "Well, thank you for having me and have a good day." I watched in disappointment as the people all plodded out of the room. I knew I had lost my opportunity.

Then I woke up. I heard the Lord speak to me saying, "If you don't go, someone else will reach the people, but it won't be for Me."

I felt the impact of that statement deeply. In my dream, I could have shared Jesus with the people, but instead the man simply entertained them. I understood that it is urgent to reach people for Christ. Their eternal destiny is at stake. Many would die not knowing Jesus as their Savior if I didn't go.

Not everyone is called to speak or minister in front of groups as I am. However, everyone is called to minister to individuals. Jesus commanded us to go into the entire world to preach the gospel, and then He promised that signs would follow all who believe. One of those signs is that those who believe would lay hands on the sick, and they would recover. (Mark 16:15-20)

In I Corinthians 2:4, Paul said, "My speech and my preaching were not with enticing words of man's wisdom, but in demonstration of the Spirit and of power." When we minister in the power of God, combined with the Word of God, we give people a living demonstration of who God is. The people are waiting for you and me to clearly represent the love and power of God. Time to go!

The Little Boy Who Couldn't Get Enough

It was quite early in my traveling ministry when I was invited to speak in a large church in Pennsylvania one fall. I wasn't feeling well that night, but I was not going to miss this opportunity to share what I knew the Lord had for the people. As I drove to the church, I prayed that the Lord would strengthen and help me. I did not realize that a young life was about to be catapulted that night.

After praise and worship were over, I shared a message taken from the story of Peter walking on the water. Then I challenged the people to "get out of the boat" and to begin to minister healing to others.

When I was finished speaking, I asked anyone who wanted to begin to pray for the sick to come to the front. My intention was to lay hands on each person and believe that God would flow through them powerfully for miracles. The Bible teaches that impartation can come from another believer. Paul spoke of this when he was encouraging his spiritual son in II Timothy 1:6. "Therefore I remind you to enflame anew the gift of God that is in you by the putting on of my hands."

EVERYDAY MIRACLES

It is important to remember that impartation is not needed for a person to minister in healing. Simple faith in the Word of God and the name of Jesus is enough to step out and see miracles. Nevertheless, the Lord does work through impartation as well.

As soon as I called those to the front who wanted prayer, a little boy of about five years of age scurried to the front. He was the first one there although no one had forced him or even encouraged him to come. He came because his heart was tender towards the Lord and those who needed healing. I was amazed to see this little tyke standing before me. I'm sure the surprise showed on my face. I laid my hands on him and asked the Lord to use him powerfully, and then I prayed for the others that had made their way to the front.

When I was finished praying for impartation, I asked those who needed healing to come up for prayer. I called this little boy who had been the first one up for the prayer of impartation to come and help me. I allowed him to lay hands on each person with me, and I helped him know what to say to each person. There were many people who needed healing, but the boy never got tired or bored. One by one, he walked with me and ministered healing. Many were healed that night, and the little boy had a large part in that.

When the service was over, the little boy looked up with big eyes and asked me eagerly, "Can we do that again on Sunday?" There was deep desire on his face, and his voice practically trembled with excitement.

I replied, "I don't know. You will have to ask your pastor. I won't be here on Sunday." I felt some disappointment that I could not continue to encourage him in his growth in healing.

God will flow powerfully through children if we will give them the opportunity and a little bit of instruction. They are naturally strong in faith. If you tell them God will heal through them, they believe it.

I often thought about that little boy in the days to come and wondered how he was doing. I prayed that someone would help him grow in his newfound ministry.

About a year later, I received a message from a woman who asked me, "Did you pray for a little boy at that church in Pennsylvania when you were there? Did you allow him to minister with you?"

I remembered this delightful child immediately and told her that I had. She then said, "I spoke to his grandmother recently. You won't believe this! She told me that he has been seeing great miracles when he prays for people ever since."

I think my heart skipped a few beats at that moment. Tears of joy and gratefulness came to my eyes. I felt deeply humbled that the Lord had allowed me to see this little boy launched. I can't wait to see him in Heaven. I have plans to give him a big high five.

No Language Barrier with God

A number of years ago, my husband and I went on a mission trip with Global Awakening, headed up by Randy Clark. We went to the beautiful nation of Brazil, a country where revival was flourishing. We were on a prayer team that ministered healing and impartation to the crowds of people who attended the services. The response was overwhelming to each call for ministry. In fact, many miracles took place and lives were changed.

At one particular meeting for leaders and pastors, Randy Clark spoke about impartation and the Biblical basis for this type of ministry. He shared many Scriptures, including Romans 1:11, in which Paul said, "I wish to impart some spiritual gift to you, that you may be established."

After he spoke, Randy Clark prayed an impartation over the prayer team of which we were a part. Most of us fell off of our seats onto the floor as the power of God come upon us. Then we were sent out into the crowds of people to lay hands on them for impartation.

The room was filled with glorious chaos. Brazilians are extremely passionate and emotional, so some of the people were crying, some were praying fervently, and some were laughing. It was difficult to hear what people were saying because of the noise coming from the people. It was a powerful time watching God touch His people.

I laid hands on one woman who was loudly wailing and prayed that the Lord would fill her and flow through her in power. It did not seem unusual to me that she was crying because the room was full of crying people. I was about to walk away when one of the other team members said, "Wait! She is saying in English, 'I repent of curses. I repent of curses.'" I went back to listen to her and she was saying those words over and over again.

In Brazil, a form of witchcraft is practiced called Macumba, and many believers were involved with that form of witchcraft before they were saved. In this form of witchcraft, curses are often sent. The New Testament plainly teaches that believers should never curse another person, but instead should bless them. Romans 12:14 tells us, "Bless those who curse you. Bless and curse not." (NAS) She had taken part in the sending of curses before she became a believer.

Believers do not need to fear being cursed because Jesus became a curse for us when He went to the cross. "Christ redeemed us from the curse of the law, being made a curse for us (for it is written cursed be everyone having been hanged on a tree)." (Gal. 2:13 NKJ)

I quietly laid hands on her again and spoke this into her spirit: "Every curse is broken through the power of Jesus and His work on the cross." Instantly, she stopped crying and an obvious peace settled down on her.

We called an interpreter over and asked him to find out if the woman knew English. When the interpreter asked her, the woman looked confused, and shook her head, indicating "No."

We realized that she had been speaking in tongues, but the language she was speaking in was English. God enabled her to speak English so that I could minister to her.

On top of that, she did not understand the words that I spoke over her. In spite of that, the Holy Spirit ministered directly to her spirit through my words.

The Lord is creative in His ability to enable us to minister successfully. I did not know her need, but He did. I have learned to put more trust in God's ability to minister than in my ability to minister. He is able.

Perfect People Not Required

One of the amazing things about God is that He is willing to flow through imperfect people. I enjoy sharing testimonies in which I do not minister perfectly because it is a reminder to me and to others that He does not need our perfection. He is looking for availability.

I was fairly new at ministering healing when I heard the Lord say a strange thing to me during our Sunday morning church service. God pointed out a woman in our church, and I thought I heard Him say, "If you will go and lay hands on that woman, I will give her 20/20 vision."

I knew that she had eye problems, but was not aware of how bad her eyes really were. Since I had never seen an eye miracle, a battle of thoughts started in my mind. Do I really want to say that to her? Surely I misunderstood the Lord. Perhaps He meant that He would give her 20/20 SPIRITUAL vision. I decided that God really must have meant 20/20 spiritual vision. I was wrong, however.

I walked up to her, and I said, "God told me that if I lay hands on you, He will give you 20/20 SPIRITUAL vision." As I lightly touched her, she flopped to the ground under God's power, and I continued to minister to other people.

While she was still on the floor, I heard her say, "Pastor Sherry, I can see out of my right eye!" I looked at her, feeling shocked, and asked, "What did you say?"

Again she said, "Pastor Sherry, I can see out of my right eye!"

Still feeling shocked, I asked, "You mean that you could not see out of your right eye before?"

She answered, "No. I was completely blind in that eye before."

She went back to her eye doctor who informed her that it was impossible for her to see out of that eye, but, in spite of that, she could clearly see. Since that day, she has continued to receive more and more healing in both of her eyes. She is able to see colors now, which she could not do formerly. She has truly been a "miracle in process".

God ministered to her in spite of my mistake and insecurity. Obedience to God, even when you are not sure of His instructions, is powerful. I have since become more secure in hearing His voice and His instructions, but I am even more secure in His love and power in spite of any mistakes that I may make.

The Same God…

When ministering healing, the enemy sometimes will inject thoughts into your mind that are contrary to God's Word. He loves to tell you that it won't work this time. He will remind you of the last time you prayed for someone and they were not healed. Satan truly hates healing and will endeavor to cause you to turn away from the healing ministry. It is important to discern the source of each thought, "catch" those contrary thoughts, and replace them with the truth. The truth is that Jesus healed everyone who came to Him, and He is willing to flow through any believer who will put their trust in Him.

On an ordinary Sunday morning, a woman brought her granddaughter up to me and said, "Look at this ganglion cyst on her wrist. Would you pray that God removes that?"

I asked her granddaughter, a precious thirteen-year-old, "Do you have pain in the ganglion cyst?"

She answered, "Lots of pain."

As soon as I placed my hand on her wrist, I heard these words go through my mind: "This cyst will not disappear instantly. It will leave gradually." It is true that sometimes healing is gradual, but I knew in my heart that the voice I heard was not God's voice. I knew it was the voice of the enemy trying to thwart my faith for an instant miracle. If I would have given into that thought, this young teen would not have experienced the power of God as she did.

Instead of agreeing with the voice in my mind, I firmly said inside my spirit, "The same God that I have seen instantly remove other cysts and growths can remove this cyst instantly as well." I didn't say anything aloud, but I spoke it in my heart to the enemy and to myself. Instantly, the cyst disappeared underneath my hand. Even though I expected the cyst to go, I still felt a surge of joy rise up inside of me.

I spoke to the teenager and said, "I believe the cyst is gone. Let's see if you can find it."

She moved her wrist around for several minutes then said, "It is gone."

I asked her, "Is the pain still there?"

She said, "No, it isn't. I can't feel anything." She continued to move her wrist around in amazement.

A few days later, her grandmother called me and said, "It was the funniest thing. On the way home, my granddaughter was talking about how the cyst disappeared, and, for just a moment, she felt a sharp pain in her wrist where the cyst had been. Then, as fast as it came, the pain left and it never came back."

The enemy had tried one more time to bring pain, but he could not prevail. The cyst never did come back, and the teen knew that she had been healed by a loving Lord.

Remember that not every thought is yours. Ask yourself whether the thought you heard lines up with God's Word and take control of what happens in your mind.

Going to Church to Get Healed

One winter, a woman in our church suddenly developed blurriness in one of her eyes. She was quite concerned and knew that a trip to her ophthalmologist was needed. As she traveled to his office, she found herself thinking of all the negative things that could be wrong.

When she arrived, she anxiously waited to see the doctor. He greeted her and called her into his office. He listened to her explanation about her eye and gave her an appropriate test. Then she received some news that she did not wish to hear.

Her doctor told her, "You have a problem with the retina in your eye. This is a disease that diabetics normally develop, but, for some reason, you have it, even though you are not diabetic. It is important that you begin to get injections in your eye or you will go blind."

The ophthalmologist explained that the injections would be painless, but the woman was quite fearful of having a needle put in her eye. Suddenly, boldness rose up in her that she did not normally have, and she answered, "No, I am not getting injections in my eye. I am going to go to church to get healed!" I can only imagine the look her doctor gave her. He tried to explain to her again how important it was to get the shots in her eyes. He assured her that they would be painless. She would not listen to his reasoning at all. He did not approve, but she walked out of his office with a determination in her heart that God would have to heal her.

The woman had been healed of many things in the past. Why would this be any different? She began to rehearse in her mind the truth of God's Word. *He paid for my healing. Why would He not heal me?*

That night, we had a service at our church, and she was there. She told me what the ophthalmologist had said, and then she repeated the words that she had used to answer him. "NO, I am not getting injections in my eye. I am going to go to church to get healed!" She was determined that she would receive healing that night. She would not have one shot. Her face told the story. She would not back down.

I laid hands on her eye and commanded healing to the retina. Immediately, she said, "The blurriness is gone! It is gone! Thank You, Jesus!" Laughter bubbled up from within her. God did it! She still did not know if the underlying cause of the blurriness was gone yet, but she was unconcerned about that. The blurriness was gone, and that was what she deemed important.

Several weeks later, she went back to her ophthalmologist. She marched right into his office expecting a good report. After he examined her, he simply shook his head, saying, "There is nothing wrong with your retina. I don't know what happened, but everything is fine now." She triumphantly walked out of his office.

That night, we had our normal Thursday night service. She walked in and said, "Guess what, Pastor Sherry?"

"What?" I asked.

"I don't need injections! My retina is healed!" The look on her face was one of "I told you so!" Then we all rejoiced right along with her.

I Feel Hands around My Neck

The presence of God is so glorious. I love to experience that presence for myself, and I love to minister His presence to others. Lives are changed, bodies are healed, and emotions are mended in His manifest presence. One woman experienced that presence in an unlikely way and in an unlikely place.

The woman sent me a message in my Facebook inbox, saying, "I have Graves' disease. Would you pray for me?" Graves' disease is an autoimmune disorder that results in the overproduction of thyroid hormones. It can manifest in bulging eyes, fatigue, muscle weakness, heart palpitations, and other symptoms. In this woman's case, she also had bone pain and weakness. At an earlier time in her life, she had part of her kidney removed because of the damage done from the Graves' disease.

I didn't know it at the time, but she was riding in her car when she sent the message. I was available to pray for her right then, so she agreed to allow me to do that. She explained later to me that, as I prayed, the presence of God came on her so strongly that she began to cry. Her husband, who was driving, was concerned and asked, "What's wrong?"

She explained, "Nothing is wrong. This lady is praying for me on Facebook, and I just can't stop crying because of God's presence."

As I prayed, she wrote to me, "I feel hands around my neck and thyroid. Wow! What is this? Now the pain is lessening around my knees and legs."

I explained, "That 'hands around your neck' feeling is the healing power of God. He is healing you."

As I continued to pray, she told me, "All the pain is gone! It is really gone!" Although I did not know it, a few days later some of the pain returned. I didn't hear from her again for a few months.

I had been invited to speak in a Spirit-filled church in Columbus, Ohio, for a series of three services that were one month apart. At the first service, while I was waiting for the meeting to begin, a woman approached me and asked, "Do you remember me? You prayed for me on Facebook for healing of Graves' disease." I only vaguely remembered that event, but I listened with great interest.

She explained, "I'm feeling much better, but some of the symptoms are still there, including a little bit of pain. I've come to the meeting for the completion of my miracle." She did not give up when the manifestation of healing was not complete, but persisted in order to receive all that God had for her.

God can heal in any way and at any time. He is not limited to time and space. However, Jesus healed by laying on of hands in the majority of cases. I love to minister in this way and greatly prefer it. When I minister in a meeting, it also gives me more time to share the good news of how Jesus healed everyone. This builds faith in those who need healing.

After I preached about the goodness of God and the price that Jesus paid for healing, many people came to the front for prayer. In this particular meeting, person after person was healed. The pastor of this church had nurtured a strong presence of God in their midst, and it was evident.

The woman with symptoms of Graves' disease was one of the people who asked for prayer. I laid hands on her and commanded the Graves' disease to leave her body, as well as every symptom of the disease. Again, all the pain left. As I normally do, I forgot all about praying for her as the days went by.

About a month later, I heard from her again. Because she had developed pneumonia, she had been admitted to the hospital. While there, the doctors ordered many blood tests. She explained to the doctors and nurses that she had Graves' disease. Her nurse answered, "No, you don't. We tested for that, and you do not have Graves' disease."

She was shocked and, once she was home, she sent me a message telling me this good news. Then she added, "I'm going to a specialist very soon, and then I will know for sure that I don't have Graves' disease any longer." She was not convinced that the disease was gone—yet.

After her visit with the specialist, she sent me one more message. The specialist had done extensive testing and, to her amazement, it was true. She said, "The testing showed that I no longer have Graves' disease. I had that for forty years, but now it is gone. Can you believe it? Forty years! God is so good. He healed me."

There have been many times when I needed to pray for people on more than one occasion in order to see the fullness of the healing manifest. Sometimes healing comes in stages. When that happens, do not become discouraged, but continue to persist in faith.

Jesus healed everyone who came to Him when He was on Earth, regardless of how long the person had been sick. Jesus is the same now as He was then. If you have received a partial healing, be extravagantly thankful for what He has done, and then believe for the completed miracle. He is able. Nothing is too hard for Him.

Herniated Disc and Spirit of Grief Gone

I had been invited to minister in a home meeting in New York on a beautiful spring day. As I drove to the meeting, I prayed in the Spirit, and, as I did, I felt a strong sense of anticipation of all that God was going to do that evening. I could hardly contain my excitement.

When I arrived, I was greeted by a large number of people who were crowded into the house. A blind woman played the keyboard and led worship. I watched her as her head bobbed up and down. She was oblivious to the people and totally focused on God. It was not long before the glory and presence of the Lord filled the room.

During that time of praise and worship, the Lord showed me a vision of the Biblical account of the four men tearing up the roof of a home so that they could get a paralyzed man to Jesus. (Mark 2:4) I knew that the Lord wanted to tear down some "roofs" or "ceilings" over people's lives that night. The "ceilings" could be wrong beliefs towards themselves or God or they could be a lack of understanding about what the Word teaches concerning healing. The "ceilings" could also be emotions that had bound the people up. I knew that when these "ceilings" were torn down, the people would be able to successfully see others set free, saved, and healed.

The Lord highlighted one woman to me in particular, and after praise and worship was over, I had her stand up. It was as if there was a Holy Ghost bull's-eye on her.

I told her the story of the four men lowering the paralyzed man to Jesus. I explained, "I believe that the Lord wants to tear down a 'ceiling' in your life that has kept you from moving into all that He has called you to do." I did not know what God wanted to do in her life more specifically that night, but I simply laid my hands on her and allowed the Lord to work. The Lord is able to move beyond my understanding as I trust Him.

As I laid hands on this dear woman, she began to weep loudly, and then she began to cough as a spirit of grief was cast out by the presence and power of God. The people in the room were obviously moved as God set her free. I did not know that the spirit of grief was there, but God did. I did not command it to go, but, without a word from me, God's powerful presence expelled it.

It was not long before her weeping turned to joy and laughter. She explained, "My husband died a decade ago, and I have had this horrible sadness and grief ever since then." She spent the next hour or so laying on the floor laughing with the joy of the Lord.

Many people were set free that night. The power of God manifested in diverse ways as some laughed and some lay quietly on the floor under God's power. Many were healed of debilitating pain. The woman who had been set free from the spirit of grief was one of them.

She had had a herniated disc in her back, and she was in much pain. I commanded, "Disc, be healed in Jesus' name. Lord, cause Your power to totally drive that out."

She began to laugh again. Between breaths, she said, "The pain is gone!"

A week later, this woman sent me a message with wonderful news. She wrote, "My grandson is nine months old, and I had never been able to hold him because of the pain in my back. Several days after you prayed for me, his mother brought him to my house for a visit. For the first time since my grandson had been born, I was able to dance around the house with him in my arms, pain-free, and full of the joy of the Lord!" How precious!

I believe that the Lord beamed with joy when He saw her dancing with her grandbaby. He cares about everything.

The woman later explained to me that she began to reach out to others who also were widows. Her sorrow had been turned to joy, and she wanted the same for others. She has been instrumental in many being set free from the crushing grief that she was set free from. God does all things well.

I Want to See Cancer Healed

There are certain miracles that have touched my heart in a special way. They are not necessarily the greatest miracles that I have seen, but they always involved an emotional response from the person receiving the healing. At times, I did not have proof of what had happened, yet, in my spirit, I knew that God had done a great work.

One snowy weekend, I was ministering at a women's conference in the mountains of Pennsylvania. It was well attended in spite of the snowy weather. The roads were treacherous, but the room was full. The women were very hungry. Many miracles took place that weekend, but there is one miracle that I will never forget.

After speaking at the first session, I asked if anyone in the room was in pain right at that moment. A young woman raised her hand. I could see the pain on her face. I asked her to stand up, and she very gingerly and slowly got to her feet. She could not turn to either side because she was in so much pain. I asked her what she needed prayer for, and she told me, "I have had a fever and pain in my bones for two weeks. My back is in so much pain that I can barely move. If I am not better by Monday, I have to have further testing." I could hear the fear in her voice.

I felt a deep concern for her, and I knew in my spirit that the extra testing would include blood tests for leukemia. I thought about her mother who was sitting nearby and how devastating it would be for her if her daughter had cancer. I remembered the trauma when my own children had serious health issues. I did not want to see anyone else go through that. I thought about what this young woman may have to go through as well. Above all, I remembered that Jesus healed all who came to Him, and I knew that His power and compassion extended to this young woman. I turned my attention away from my concern, and I turned it to His love and power.

I reminded the young woman that Jesus paid for her healing, and then I laid hands on her. I often have people in my meetings help with the healing ministry by having them say, "This healing belongs to her because of what Jesus did!" I saw that modeled by healing minister Roger Sapp and it is very effective. I had the ladies say that with me, and then I commanded the symptoms to leave her body in Jesus' name.

I was elated to see the stress on her face melt away and a huge smile form. I eagerly asked, "How do you feel?"

She moved her back all around for a while, and then she said, "There is no pain at all." Then she added, "I feel as if the fever has left as well." She continued to give me this big grin. She continued to grin the entire evening. I will never forget the look on her face.

She returned to the meeting the next day, and I watched her during praise and worship. She joyfully raised her hands to the King who had healed her, and she worshipped Him with all of her heart. She no longer had a problem with moving around because the pain and fever were totally gone. As I preached that day, I noticed that the smile never left her face. I felt great joy to see what the Lord had done in her life.

There is a "rest of the story" though. The night before I left for the women's conference, a few people from my church decided to pray for me. As they began to pray, in my heart I whispered, "Lord, I just want to see cancer healed this weekend."

As soon as I silently whispered that, I heard a woman pray for me, saying, "Lord, give her the desire of her heart this weekend." My spirit leapt inside of me. I knew that God had heard my prayer. Seeing cancer healed was the desire of my heart.

I had to drive home the day after the meetings were over on icy roads through the mountains. I did not enjoy that at all, but my thoughts kept returning to the young woman who formerly had pain in her bones. I could not get her smiling face out of my mind. It is hard to express how grateful I was to God for allowing me to be a part of her miracle. Even now it makes me smile.

Even though there was no doctor's report, my heart rejoiced that God had touched this beautiful, young woman who was so in love with Jesus. You never know what surgery or sickness may be averted when you minister healing to someone. Our part is to touch people's lives with compassion and allow the Lord to bring healing to them.

Led by a Word and a Vision

It is very humbling to me when the Lord specifically directs a person to one of my meetings. I know that I am completely dependent on Him, and without Him nothing of value takes place.

On one occasion, I arrived early to a church where I was scheduled to speak at a women's healing encounter. When I walked into the sanctuary, I saw a woman, a teenager, and several children sitting in the back row. I walked back to greet them, and the woman said, "Are you Sherry Evans?"

I answered, "Yes, I am. I am so glad to meet you."

She introduced her daughter and grandchildren to me, and then she said, "I was praying several days ago, and I heard the Lord say the name of this church where you are speaking. I was puzzled because I did not know where the church was located, and I certainly did not know why the Lord spoke its name to me." She went on, "Several hours later, I opened up my Facebook, and up popped a poster of this meeting at this church. I just knew that God was up to something big in my life."

Equally puzzled, I asked, "Do you have a Facebook friend who attends this church? How did the poster get on your timeline?"

She answered, "No, I don't know how it got there. It was just there. I knew that God was leading me to come to this meeting."

The story gets more interesting than that. When her teenage daughter came home from high school, the woman said, "I had the strangest experience today. The Lord spoke the name of a church to me, and when I looked on Facebook, I saw that the church was having a healing meeting in a few days. Come and look at the poster."

They opened up Facebook to look at the poster, and the daughter said, "Mom, I had a vision of that poster today at school. It was superimposed over a door." I would have loved to have seen the expressions on their faces as they relayed what God had shown each of them independently.

All I could think about was how awesome God is. Not only did he lead this woman in a creative, unusual way, but He was allowing me to be a part of her miracle. These are the kinds of things that cause me to be amazed.

The mother, daughter, and grandchildren had arrived at that meeting as early as possible. They were determined to receive what God had for them. The mother came up for prayer after the message, explaining, "I have been dealing with so much anxiety that I haven't been able to sleep." Her faith was strong to receive that evening, and, as I touched her, she knew that she had been set free. She responded with loud praises to God.

The Lord is intimately involved in our lives. He knows what we struggle with, and He knows how to help us. Our part is to trust Him with all of our hearts and to continue to thank Him for what He is doing. We must be sensitive to the words that He speaks to our spirits, and we must be careful to obey Him.

He will often flow through the most unlikely person to bring healing or freedom. He delights in using those who seem insignificant in this world. I have often felt as if I am one of those "unlikely, insignificant" ones. When we are weak, He is strong.

Never Too Old

On one occasion, I was invited to conduct a healing service for a women's event in Ohio. With great anticipation, I arrived at the meeting early and was met there by a "fire cracker" of a woman. She seemed to be in constant motion, and as soon as she saw me, she began to loudly declare, "I've been looking forward to this meeting so much. Praise God! I know God is going to do something awesome. Glory! Healing is so wonderful. Praise the Lord! Oh, He is so good!" It felt as if she had twice the energy that I had, and I felt invigorated just being around her. I didn't know it at the time, but she was eighty-two years old.

I spoke that night about the woman with the issue of blood. This Biblical woman received a miracle by reaching out to Jesus for her healing. Jesus did not need to pray and ask the Father if healing was His will. In fact, He could not have asked God for direction because He was unaware that the woman was reaching for Him. In fact, Jesus never had to ask God if His will was to heal the sick because He knew that it always was with no exceptions. The very nature of God is healing. We can reach out to Him and receive.

After I was done speaking, the eighty-two-year-old "fire cracker" came up for prayer. She told me that she had pain in her arm, and so I reached out and touched her. She began to scream and shake violently just as if she had touched an electric wire, and then she landed on the floor. Later, when she got up, she said, "It felt like a bolt of electricity went through me. I've never felt anything like that before." Because I was praying for someone else at that time, I forgot to ask her if the pain was gone.

About six weeks later, I received a message from a woman explaining that she had seen the eighty-two-year-old "fire cracker". I knew that the "fire cracker's" words were speckled with, "Praise the Lord" and, "Glory to God." I knew that she would appear to be in constant motion. I could imagine her saying, "Praise God! God is so good! The pain never came back. I am completely healed." The woman told me that the "fire cracker" told her exactly that. She had no more pain.

I called the "fire cracker" on the phone to find out more about what she had experienced. Her voice was full of excitement and vigor, and she seemed to talk a mile a minute. She said, "Glory to God! That pain in my arm had been caused by tumors. I had received prayer before many times, but the pain always came back. Not this time! God healed me. Praise Jesus! Oh, I just love Him."

Jesus never turned anyone away because they were too old to be healed. He never explained to anyone that pain was their lot in life because of their age. He healed them all! Reach out today to Jesus as the woman with the issue of blood reached out to Him and receive as she did.

I-I-I Don't Know Why I'm Shaking

Many times during a meeting, the Lord will heal people before I have an opportunity to pray for them. Their faith reaches out to Jesus, and they receive healing just like the woman with the issue of blood reached out to Jesus in the Bible. Sometimes people are healed as they sit in their seats or as they walk to the front of the room.

This happened on one occasion when I was ministering in a church near Columbus, Ohio. After I preached the Word, I invited those wanting healing to come to the front for prayer. I had already prayed for several people when I noticed a young woman who had come from her seat in the back of the church and had sat down in the front row. The reason why I noticed her was because she was shaking from head to foot.

I love it when the Lord gives me a word of knowledge about someone, but in this case I heard nothing. Since I did not know why she was shaking, I asked, "Why are you shaking?"

She said to me, "I-I-I don't know why I am shaking."

I felt even more confused, so I asked, "Is this part of your physical condition?"

I noticed a little bit of fear on her face as she told me, "No."

At that point I realized that she was experiencing the presence of God on her, and that was what was causing her to shake. She had never experienced the power of God in this way before and truly did not know what was happening to her. I asked, "Would you like prayer?"

She answered me with some difficulty because she was shaking so much. She said, "Yes, please. I have hepatitis C, and lately my liver enzymes have been sky high. My doctor has ordered a biopsy. I'm so scared." Tears welled up in her eyes as she told me this.

I was not sure if she actually still needed prayer from me because the Holy Spirit was already touching her, but I laid my hand on her anyway, and I agreed with God that healing was taking place. Instantly, all the shaking stopped. I saw a new peace form on her face. I knew in my spirit that she was healed.

Several weeks later, I received a call from someone from the church where I had ministered. I was not able to answer the phone when he called, but he had left a message. I noticed the excitement in his voice as he spoke and wondered what he was going to tell me. He said, "Remember that young woman sitting in the front row with Hepatitis C? Well, she went back to her doctor, and he decided to retest her liver enzymes. They were completely normal! I knew something special was going to happen that day, and it did. Praise God!"

I went back to that church to minister several months later and a woman caught me after the meeting and asked if she could speak to me. "Sure," I responded. It is not unusual for people to want to speak to me after a service, so I did not know that she had something very significant to tell me.

She said, "I don't know if you remember me, but you prayed for my granddaughter a few months ago. She was the one with hepatitis C. Well, her doctor ordered a new scan on her liver, and he said that it looked totally different. She has a new, healthy liver now!"

All I could do was to thank God for His amazing goodness. I rejoiced for this dear young lady who received His healing. Even though I expect healing when I pray for people, I have never lost my sense of amazement when they are healed. God had given this woman a creative miracle. He has great compassion for each of us, and He could not wait until I was available to pray. He began the healing process without my involvement, and I came into agreement with what He was doing.

The Case of the Mistaken Diagnosis

For a number of months, I had been conducting a monthly meeting in an apartment building for those with limited incomes. Even though the people were open to hearing about Jesus as Savior, it felt as if I were hitting a brick wall in presenting Jesus as Healer. Every month I would share from the Word the simple truth that Jesus paid for our healing as well as our salvation. Since Jesus healed all who came to Him when He was on Earth, it was God's will to heal all who now came to Him. They listened, but the truth seemed to go in one ear and out the other. Although a few people had experienced healing as I prayed, they did not seem to adopt their own faith for healing.

A breakthrough came when we had a Christmas party for those in the building who wanted to attend. People in the apartment building stared as a woman came with an old grocery cart and helped us take loads of gift baskets up to our meeting room. It took several trips with that rickety grocery cart to get all the gift baskets to the meeting room. Soon people began to trickle into the room with curious expressions on their faces.

I passionately spoke about the best Christmas gift of all, Jesus Christ, and the people listened with interest. It brings me great joy to share the simple gospel of Jesus with those who are yet to know Him. Afterwards, I urged them by saying, "The Lord is waiting with open arms for you to receive Him as your Savior. Do it today. If you would like to give your life to Jesus, raise your hand." Hands went up all over the room, and I was honored to lead them straight to the loving arms of the Father.

I went on to explain, "You have received God's Christmas gift of salvation, but He has another gift for you. That gift is one of healing. He paid for it, and all you need to do is to receive it." Then a team from my church and I prayed for those who needed healing. A number of miracles took place that day. One of the miracles involved a former Lutheran social worker and lay preacher.

He called me over to where he was seated, pointed to his ear, and said, "I have a loud roaring in my ear. Would you pray for me?"

I lightly touched his ear and prayed, "Lord, touch this ear and drive out this roar." A huge smile came on his face.

"How is it now?" I asked.

"Much better," he said. I prayed once more. "It is almost gone," he told me. If his smile could have gotten any bigger, it did at that moment.

I called over a woman who was learning to flow in healing and told her, "Now you pray for that ear."

She barely got the prayer out before he said, with amazement in his voice, "My ear is completely quiet now! Wow! The roar is completely gone!" He was not expecting his ear to be healed even though he had asked for prayer.

Several months later, I was again at this apartment complex. After sharing the Word, I asked if anyone wanted prayer. The Lutheran man spoke up and told me, "I know that God can heal me because the tinnitus in my ear is completely gone since you prayed for me. It never came back either. Because of that, I want to ask you to pray for something else. My hand and arm are numb. Would you pray for that?"

I assumed that he had neuropathy, so I went over and lightly touched his fingers while saying, "Neuropathy, go from his hand and arm in Jesus' name."

After I was done, he said, "Your fingers are cold."

I answered, "Yes, they are."

He quickly added, "No, you don't understand. I have not been able to feel anything in this hand for seven years!" He kept rubbing his hand on his pants, saying, "I can feel the material in my pants. I haven't been able to feel that for seven years!"

He repeatedly rubbed his hand on his pants and looked up at me with that big smile on his face. "There is only one thing wrong," he said. "I didn't have neuropathy. My hand was numb as a result of a stroke that I had seven years ago." He still had the huge smile on his face, and his eyes twinkled like he was telling me a funny joke.

Even though I had diagnosed his problem incorrectly and commanded the wrong condition to leave, the Lutheran man and I had reached out in faith to God for his healing, and we were not disappointed. God is bigger than our mistakes. It is not the accuracy of our words that bring healing, but it is faith in the name of Jesus that brings healing. God can work in spite of our mistakes if we will put our trust in Him. As I often say, "Our perfection is not required."

The Ten-Year-Long Migraine

On one spring morning, I was speaking at an apartment complex church service when in burst a woman and her small dog. "This is my guardian," she laughingly said as she pointed to her dog. She sat down, listened with interest, and added her own humorous comments. Gales of laughter rang out from the others in the room. I spoke about Jesus' visit to Mary and Martha's home. Martha was busy serving, but Mary sat right down at Jesus' feet and listened to Him teach. Martha was upset at Mary for not helping her, but Jesus would not allow Mary's deep desire to be with Him to be taken from her. Mary understood that Jesus desired her as a friend, not just a servant.

After I was finished speaking, I spoke to the group and said, "Let's pray for everyone in this apartment building that they will come to know Jesus as their Savior and their friend as Mary did."

As we prayed, the woman with the dog began to pray and finished by saying, "Please, Lord, take away this migraine. It hurts so bad."

I quickly walked over to her and asked, "May I pray for you?"

She had never been to our service and had never met me before, so I caught her by surprise. She didn't expect someone to actually minister the healing power of God to her right then. She looked up at me with wide eyes and said, "Yes, please do."

I commanded, "Migraine, go from her in Jesus' name."

I saw her eyes get even wider. "It's going!" she said. "I've had that migraine for ten years! It started after I was in a car accident in which I hurt my neck, and it has been there ever since."

Since there had been an injury to her neck, I also placed my hand on her neck and said, "Trauma, you go from her neck in Jesus' name."

"Wow! I felt something lift off of my neck! Oh, my! I have no more pain!" she excitedly told me. She moved her neck and head all around to try to find the pain, but she could not find it. The sheer power of God removed a ten-year-old migraine. I can't imagine the agony of living so long with that kind of pain.

She explained, "I no longer live in these apartments, although I did years ago. This morning, I woke up and suddenly remembered that there was church here on Wednesday mornings. For some reason, I felt an urge to come." I knew the reason why she felt such an urge to come to church. It was her day for a miracle. The Holy Spirit was tugging on her heart.

I asked, "How far away do you live?"

She answered, "All the way across town. When I got here, I asked the woman at the desk if I could come to church." She needed to ask to come inside because this was a locked building. "She told me that I could."

"I got to the meeting just in time," she exclaimed.

She left that meeting with her "guardian" and a glow on her face. She continued to laugh and joke with everyone, but the expression on her face was different. God had set her free from ten years of pain.

The Lady in Red

As I was driving to a home meeting in Ohio one evening, I began to praise and worship God with great joy. Suddenly, the Lord interrupted me with a quick vision of a woman wearing red. I did not see her face in the vision, but I had a clear image of her bright red outfit. I felt sure that the Lord was showing me someone He intended to heal that night. With great excitement, I began to pray for all those who would be in attendance and especially for the "lady in red" as I drove.

When I arrived, I walked into a crowded room of chattering, joyful people. I looked around for the "lady in red" but I didn't see her at first. *Where is she?* I thought. Then, right before we started, a woman walked in wearing the red outfit I had seen in my vision.

I shared a message with the group about how God instructed the Israelites to make a serpent and to put it on a "pole". If anyone was bitten by a snake, they were to look at that serpent, and they would be healed. (Numbers 21:7-9) They could not focus on their symptoms and the snake on the cross at the same time. Instead, they needed to turn their attention from their bite and firmly put it on the snake on the pole. This was a clear picture of how Jesus would be made a curse for us. He took our sicknesses on Himself. If we look to Him as our Healer, we will also be healed. It is imperative that we focus on Him.

After I was finished speaking, I looked at the "lady in red" and asked, "Did you come to the meeting tonight because you need healing?"

She said, "Yes, I have. There is something wrong with the connective tissue in my mouth. My doctor has scheduled me for a biopsy." Whenever anyone hears the word "biopsy" there can be a measure of fear.

I explained, "I asked you if you needed healing because I had a vision of a woman dressed in red while I was driving here tonight. Since you are the only one here wearing red, the vision was of you. God desires to heal you."

Visions and words of knowledge build faith in those who are recipients of them. However, God wants to heal everyone whether they receive a word of knowledge or whether they do not. Words of knowledge are like a personal invitation from the captain to a meal during a cruise. The fact is, however, the meals come free to everyone whether they receive a personal invitation or not.

In order to understand her situation more completely, I asked, "Are you in pain?"

"Oh, yes. I can barely touch my face," she replied. I walked over to her and prayed a quick prayer.

I asked, "How is the pain now?"

She began to feel her face with her hands. "I can't feel any pain now at all. It's gone!" she answered with amazement in her voice.

As the meeting went on, many more were healed, and one lovely, young woman led the people in singing songs of praise in between the miracles. It was a night that left the people full of joy in the Spirit. Some said that they continued to be giddy and filled with joy the next day. We had fun in the Lord that night.

I didn't hear from the "lady in red" for a number of days. Then she contacted me with an exciting report. She said, "When I went back to my doctor, he was amazed. He checked the connective tissue in my mouth, and he told me that there was no longer any indication of disease." Here is the clincher: The doctor simply said, "All I can say is that you seem to have made a 'miraculous' recovery. There is no need for a biopsy any longer."

She made a miraculous recovery because the God of miracles healed her. What a great God!

The Strange Case of Numbness

A teenage girl hobbled into our church on crutches during one of our evening services. I looked at her with curiosity, but I waited until the meeting was over to speak to her. "What happened?" I asked.

She answered in an evasive way: "I don't know how, but I hurt my leg, and I'm in so much pain."

I offered to pray for her, and she said, "Yes, please pray for me."

I laid my hand on her leg and said, "Lord, heal this and drive out the pain. Heal the cause of the pain."

Her eyes widened as she looked at me. I could tell by her grimace that the pain had gotten worse instead of better. "What is happening?" I asked.

She struggled through her words, saying, "When you touched my leg, it went completely numb, and the pain is excruciating now."

It's a spirit of infirmity. No problem. It will go. I was unconcerned, although I was a little confused.

"Spirit of infirmity, go from this leg," I commanded. I looked at her face, expecting her to relax as the pain left, but her expression remained the same. "How is it now?" I asked.

"It's the same," she answered.

What is going on here? I don't understand. Did I make a mistake in how I prayed for her? Lord, help!

I was new at ministering healing then, and this teen had only been at our church a few times. A little bit of fear began to enter into my heart. Since then I have learned that I can trust God even when the unusual happens. I had released God's power to her, and His power would continue to bring healing.

The next day, I called her mother to ask how the teen was doing. "She is still in a lot of pain. I took her to a chiropractor this morning and he refused to touch her. The damage is that bad. He said that her back, hip, and leg are damaged."

I continued to feel some concern for this young girl, and I prayed for her often during the day. However, with God there are many "suddenlys" and this young girl was about to experience one.

Just about twenty-four hours later to the minute, the teen called me on the phone and shouted with an excited voice, "Guess what, Pastor Sherry, just now, all the numbness left and all the pain left. I am completely healed!" I could hear her laughing with sheer joy and relief.

The next day, she came to church without her crutches, and she worshiped her heart out. God had done it. He had done what He had promised.

God desires all to be healed; it is also true that our enemy wants no one to be healed. The Word expresses it well when it states: "....how God anointed Jesus of Nazareth with the Holy Spirit and with power, and He went about doing good and healing all that were oppressed of the devil, for God was with Him." (Acts 10:38) The book of Revelation tells us that there is a time when the devil comes down "having great wrath, knowing that His time is short." (Rev. 12:2) The devil did not want this teen free from pain, but God had the final word.

When you minister healing or when you are receiving ministry for healing, continue to believe God no matter what the immediate results appear to be. Appearances are deceptive. Jesus is our Healer, and He is faithful.

The "Walking Time Bomb"

In our church, we have a woman who the doctors called the "Walking Time Bomb". She was given that name because she had a noncancerous tumor in her head that would explode if she hit her head hard enough. She lived in fear for many years that she would slip on ice or snow and hit her head. Almost thirty years prior, a shunt had been placed in her head to drain the tumor. The shunt complicated her life because it would sometimes slip out of place and cause pain.

During one of our Thursday night services, I suddenly thought of the tumor in the woman's head. This may have been a word of knowledge that came as an impression. I turned to her and asked, "Do you still have that tumor?"

"Yes, I do," she said.

I laid hands on her head and commanded, "Tumor, go from her head in Jesus' name."

With a whimsical voice, she said, "My head is getting hot!" Then she began to laugh as the Holy Spirit touched her. She joyfully said, "I feel so good!" In His presence is fullness of joy.

Several weeks later, the woman went to her ophthalmologist for an eye exam. Because the tumor was so close to her eye, he always did x-rays to determine the size of the tumor. She sat down and waited for him to come into the room without even thinking about the prayer for healing that she had received.

After a time, the doctor came into the room where the woman was waiting and said, "I don't understand this, but the tumor is gone."

The woman was astonished and asked, "What did you say?"

He repeated, "The tumor is gone."

She left the office feeling like she was floating on a cloud. The feelings of euphoria came from joy and absolute amazement. Her mother was in the waiting room, and when she saw her, she repeated what the doctor had said: "Mom, the tumor is gone!"

Her mother said the same thing her daughter had said. In shock, she asked, "What did you say?"

The former "walking time bomb" repeated, "The tumor is gone!" Now they both walked out of the office feeling like they were floating on a cloud.

The next Thursday night, she walked into the church and said, "Guess what. The tumor is gone!" Joy broke out all over the room.

We have many people in our church who pray for healing. For this reason, I don't know how many times she had received prayer for the tumor. It is possible that I had prayed for her in the past as well. I don't know why the healing occurred on this occasion, but it did. Continue to trust God for your healing.

The Healing Seed

I love to travel and minister, so when I received an invitation to speak at a church near Columbus, I was elated, as usual. I felt great anticipation inside as I drove to the meeting.

When I got there, I entered the building and glanced around. The room was filled with smiling, chattering people. It did not take me long to feel right at home.

There was a strong presence of God during the praise and worship time, and I felt the freedom of the Spirit in the room. *This is going to be a great meeting*, I thought.

After I was done preaching, I gave a word of knowledge for healing of neuropathy in feet. It was simply an impression in my spirit that God wanted to heal that condition. I asked anyone in the room who had neuropathy to come to the front. I don't remember how many came up, but I do remember three people vividly.

I had already preached the Word showing that healing was paid for by Jesus when He went to the whipping post. I also had shared stories of other cases of neuropathy that I had seen healed, and the various ways that I had seen healing manifest. Finally, I reminded the group that miracles are instant, but healing is sometimes gradual. I wanted people to continue to believe for healing, even if there was not an instant manifestation.

I walked up to the first man and commanded the neuropathy to go. I said, "Check it out. Is the pain less, the same or more now?"

In response, he began to stomp his feet as hard as he could, saying with a smile, "I don't feel any pain or numbness anymore at all. It is all gone."

Then I prayed for another man with neuropathy in his feet. I asked, "Is anything happening that you can tell?"

He said, "Not that I can tell. Everything seems to be the same." I reminded him to keep thanking God for healing him and went on to the next person.

Last of all, I prayed for a woman with neuropathy. I asked her the same thing that I had asked the others. "How do your feet feel now? Is there any difference?"

She answered, "I can't tell any difference right now, but I KNOW that I am healed. Praise God! He is faithful!" Faith and confidence resonated in her voice as she continued to thank God for her healing.

About an hour later, I walked out of the meeting with a spring in my steps. Joy surged through my heart. *Thank You, Lord, for touching these people. You are wonderful. I am so blessed to be a part of this.*

As I was walking to my car, I heard a man shout, "Hey, Sherry!" I looked around, and I saw that it was the man I had prayed for with neuropathy in his feet who had not seen any change after I prayed. From across the parking lot, he shouted, "Hey, my feet feel pretty good!" He had an amazed smile on his face. At a later date, the pastor confirmed to me that he had been completely healed. The neuropathy was gone, and it never came back.

I went back to that church a month later to conduct another meeting. A woman raised her hand and asked, "May I share a testimony?"

"Sure," I answered.

She said, "Last month, I received prayer for neuropathy in my feet, but nothing happened." Then she added, "But I KNEW that I was healed. Several weeks ago, I was out shopping and I noticed something. My feet did not hurt! I had no numbness in them anymore. I don't even know when the healing manifested, but it did. I'm healed! Praise God!" The room erupted with loud clapping and praise to God. We all rejoiced with her that day.

I love it when healing is instant. Sometimes, however, healing is more gradual or it is delayed. It is important to continue believing the Word in spite of what you see in the moment. Healing is like a seed that is planted in the ground. It has to grow up. When the seed has been planted through healing ministry, don't dig it up through unbelief. Instead, continue to thank God for the manifestation of the healing.

The Four for One Miracle

I was ministering at one of our earliest healing services in my church when a precious, elderly couple walked to the front of the room. The husband stood behind his wife as she said in a frustrated voice, "I want to be able to hear clearly again. I have 40% hearing loss in one ear, and I am always asking people to repeat what they are saying."

This was the first time that I had ever prayed for a hearing problem, but I ministered the same way that I would pray for any other condition. I gently touched her ear, commanded healing, and then waited for just a moment. Suddenly, her face lit up. I asked her, "What is happening?"

She said, "I think I can hear perfectly out of this ear now." I tested her hearing by softly clicking my fingers from farther and farther distances away, and she heard each one.

I turned to her husband and asked, "Could she have heard that before?"

He answered me loudly, "No, she couldn't." He paused a moment and shouted with a humorous look on his face, "Hey, wait a minute! I couldn't have heard that before either." Those who were watching began to laugh.

His wife jumped into the conversation and said, "That's for sure. His hearing was worse than mine."

God had healed his ears as I was praying for his wife's ear. He was beside himself with joy, and he said, "These are the kind of services that I love."

I wanted to shout out, "Me too."

Another couple in the meeting was watching with interest and decided that it was their turn for hearing miracles. Seeing the first couple's miracles caused their own faith to rise up. They walked to the front of the room and explained that they also had hearing loss.

I prayed for the husband first, and his hearing improved instantly. However, when I laid hands on his wife, nothing seemed to happen. I was a little puzzled, but I listened for special instructions from the Holy Spirit. I sensed that He was saying to have her husband lay hands on her ears.

I told the husband what the Holy Spirit had instructed him to do. Even though he didn't say a word, as soon as he touched her ears, they opened up, and she could hear clearly.

In a matter of a few minutes, God performed four hearing miracles, but He did not do it the same way each time. I have learned to expect the unexpected when ministering healing. Healing is truly an adventure.

The Unclaimed Word of Knowledge

The presence of God was intense during a service at the church that my husband and I pastor one Sunday morning. We had worshiped God with all of our hearts, and the power of God was flowing. Suddenly, I had an impression that someone had pain in the middle of their back. I did not know what was causing the pain, but I gave the word with the information that I had.

No one responded to the word of knowledge, but a woman in our church spoke up and explained, "I have heat in the middle of my back." At first I thought that she was receiving a healing in her back, so I asked a few people sitting close to her to lay hands on her to facilitate God's healing power. Although they did lay hands on her, nothing seemed to change in her back or her body. Hmmm… I wondered what was happening.

Then the woman with heat in her back said, "I think that this is the same word of knowledge that you had, but in a different form." A "light bulb" went on in my mind. Learning to flow in the gifts of the Spirit is a learning process, and we are all in the Spirit's "school".

I asked again, "Does anyone here have pain in the middle of their back?" Everyone looked at me with blank stares on their faces. Since no one claimed the word of knowledge, we went on with the meeting.

After the service was over, my husband and I went to a local Mexican restaurant to eat. My cell phone rang as we were driving home. I answered the phone to hear a woman in our church speak with a weak, labored voice. She was obviously in a lot of pain. She said, "I was the woman with pain in my back during church, but it was only slight when you gave the word of knowledge. When I got home, though, the pain became horrendous. When my daughter checked the spot where the pain was, she said that she thought I had shingles."

I was puzzled. Why didn't she respond to the word of knowledge? When I asked her, she said, "I thought that the pain was from my bra. I thought maybe it was stuck in my back, and I didn't want to say that. I was too embarrassed. "

I giggled a little to myself, and then I prayed, "Lord, remove every bit of pain. Shingles, go from her body in Jesus' name."

I heard the relief in her voice as she said, "The pain is gone! The pain is completely gone!" The pain had left instantly.
 Oh, the mercy of God! He healed her in spite of her mistake and lack of response. She thanked me for praying, and we hung up with grateful hearts to the Lord.

About an hour later, she called me and gave me more exciting news. She said, "My daughter just checked, and now the rash is gone as well! Praise God! God is so good. I don't know how I would have been able to continue packing with that horrible pain." She had recently lost her husband and was in the process of moving. She was busy packing up for the move and would have been hindered if she had to deal with shingles.

I often receive words of knowledge through an impression. Others receive words of knowledge by feeling pain in the spot where the person has pain. Some even feel heat to indicate a word of knowledge. Some have visions, see words or hear words. As we cooperate with the Holy Spirit, He teaches us how to flow with what He is doing.

I have found that God is more concerned with people being healed than He is about His ministers looking like they never make a mistake. If you have a word of knowledge but when you give it no one responds, remember that the person it was intended for may have been too embarrassed to speak out. It is important to speak the word that you hear and leave the results to God.

Unstuck!

God is truly amazing. If we could see Him as He is our lives would be forever changed. There is no sickness, no emotional wound, and no psychological condition that is bigger than God. The One who created the universe is awesome beyond words. For those who see Him as great and mighty, He will show Himself to be great and mighty.

While holding a healing service in Ohio one evening, a woman came up to the front where I was standing and said in a desperate tone of voice, "I wonder if you can help me."

She had a troubled, anxious look on her face, and I wondered what kind of help she wanted. I began to explain that I would pray for her, but I could not do any counseling at that moment. There were many things running through my mind. I even wondered if she was going to ask me for money.

I asked, "What is it that you need the Lord to do for you?"

She answered, "I'm stuck, and I don't know how to get unstuck. I can't hear God or feel God. I feel no emotion at all. I feel totally numb emotionally. I am dead inside."

Her face reflected what she told me. She looked emotionally

dead. I told her that I believed that God was able to set her free right at that moment. God can do what hours and hours of counseling cannot. A glimmer of hope came into her eyes.

I laid hands on her and prayed a simple prayer. I said, "Lord, 'unstuck' her!" It was not a deep prayer, but sometimes the simplest of prayers, prayed in faith, are what God wants. He desires our faith more than our fancy, intelligent prayers. What happened next was astounding.

Her eyes got huge, and she said, "I feel heat in my heart. Now I feel heat in my stomach." Her voice got louder and louder as she said the words to me. I watched her as God delivered her without anyone knowing what was happening. She yawned widely several times, and I knew that tormenting spirits were leaving her.

All of a sudden, her face lit up, and a look of excitement took the place of the dead look. She fell to her knees and screamed out, "I'm unstuck! I'm unstuck! She unstuck me. You all must come up here and get prayer. If she could 'unstick' me, she can do anything."

I quickly and urgently said, "No, no, no! God 'unstuck' you. It was God!" The room erupted with laughter.

I knew that only God had the power to set her free. All I did was touch her. I didn't even know what to say. I wanted everyone in the room to understand that God did it, not me.

There are times when I have prayed for people and seen them set free instantly from depression, anxiety, and a host of other emotional issues. There have also been times when the instant freedom did not come. My constant prayer is for increase in this area.

A little later in the meeting, I asked if anyone wanted to come up and help me minister. The woman who had previously said that she was stuck eagerly volunteered. I had her lay hands on a woman's knees as I prayed for her healing from arthritic pain. The arthritic pain was so bad that she could barely walk. After a few minutes of prayer, the knee pain was completely gone.

I spoke to the entire room and said, "Healing is a great adventure that you go on with the Holy Spirit. He will surprise you in the way that He does things at times. Isn't this fun? Are you having fun?"

The "unstuck" woman looked up at me with absolute joy on her face and shouted, "I sure am having fun!" God does all things well.

The Little Girl with Braids

I have always had a deep desire to minister without embarrassing people. I have found that the Lord has honored that desire to an amazing degree in my ministry.

One Thursday evening at church, I saw a vision of a little girl with braids in her hair. I could tell that she was about six to eight years old with dark hair and dancing eyes. She was as cute as could be. Since that is all that the Lord had shown me, I asked every woman present who had worn braids at that age to come to the front of the room. I laid hands on each one of them and asked the Lord to do what He wanted to do in them. The Lord did not show me any details of what He intended to do that night, but I trusted Him to perform what each woman needed.

The results were dramatic. Several women landed on the floor under the power of God. Some laughed, and some saw visions. To some people, the event may have looked like chaos, with some women laughing and some falling on the floor. To God, however, this was perfect order. It was His order. God was not finished yet, though. The Lord wanted to minister to one woman in particular. As I touched her, she fell to the ground and began to gently cough and sigh. I knew that the

Lord was setting her free from demonic torment. I sat down beside her on the floor and whispered in her ear, commanding every unclean spirit to leave her in Jesus' name. The Lord touched her so gently that no one knew she was receiving deliverance. It was truly precious to see how gently the Lord was setting her free. She got up from the floor with a new joy and freedom.

At first, I did not know the connection between her deliverance and the braids in her hair. Later, she explained the connection to me. She said, "You see, I was molested as a child, and I would have worn braids at the time I was molested. I was that little girl in the vision." God set her free from much torment that night.

The Lord had only revealed one thing to me, and that was the picture of the girl with braids. I did not need to know the details of her need. God went beyond my natural understanding. All I needed to do was release God's power to her. The Lord gently ministered to her in a way that did not expose her or embarrass her.

A large part of growing in ministry is learning to rest in God's ability to heal and to set people free. It is in resting, not striving, that God's power flows the most powerfully. He wants to heal His children far more than we want to see them healed, and He knows exactly how to do it.

I Feel Your Hand

I was privileged to minister a number of times over several years at a church in a rural area of Ohio. Every invitation is exciting to me, but these invitations were especially exciting because there is a drug rehabilitation center in the church. I love to minister to those who truly are in need of the power of God, as these men were. I love the honesty of those who know they have needs, as those in a drug rehabilitation center would be. On top of that, I knew in my spirit that these men at the center were going to be world-changers for God. I considered it a privilege to be allowed to minister to them.

On one of the occasions that I was there, however, the men in the center were not able to attend the service. After the meeting was over, I continued to speak to people as they came to me. As we were talking, I looked up and saw the men from the rehabilitation center file through the door and rush to where I was standing. They had returned from a previous commitment, and they were hungry for a touch from God. Patiently, they waited for their turn to receive prayer. Many were impacted, but one man stood out in my mind. He said, "I need prayer for my back. I have no bones at all in the lower part of my back. All I have is metal back there." I did not even know that a back with no bones was possible.

As I prayed for him, a grimace formed on his face. I asked him what was happening; he said, "I'm feeling a lot of pressure and pain in my back that was not there before." On occasion, I have seen pain get worse before a person is healed.

I continued to pray, but he interrupted me and said with great amazement, "I feel your hand on my back!"

I asked, "You couldn't feel that before I prayed?" I was as surprised as he was.

He told me, "No, all the nerve endings in my lower back were completely dead! I couldn't feel anything at all before. Nothing."

In a few minutes, all feeling had returned to his back, and, when it did, all of the pain and the pressure disappeared as well. His eyes were wide with amazement. God restored the dead nerve endings even though I had not prayed for that.

Miracles Are Contagious

On one occasion, when I was at the church that hosted a drug rehabilitation center, the men had come in early that morning from an event the night before. Although they were tired, they were all sitting in the front several rows of the church bright and early for the service. As I began to speak, they struggled to focus on what I was saying because they were so tired.

I spoke that day about miracles. I encouraged the people to begin to step out in the Word and pray for healing for others. In the course of this, I told many stories of the miracles that I had seen on the streets and in churches. I wanted to inspire the people that they could see the same.

There was a man who lived in the rehabilitation center who considered himself an atheist in attendance at this meeting. At first, he was disinterested. In fact, he didn't believe a word I said. God has a way of getting people's attention, however. As he continued to watch the miracles, and as he listened to the testimonies, his interest began to be aroused. Could it possibly be true? Eventually, his skepticism was changed to faith, and his faith changed to a deep repentance. Of course, I knew nothing about this as I was speaking.

The next time I came to minister at that church, the man who thought he was an atheist asked if he could speak with me. Of course, I wanted to hear what he had to say. I still did not know that he had considered himself an atheist. He told me, "After the last meeting, I was so stirred in my heart. I found a time to be by myself and I cried out to God. I asked Him to forgive me for my disbelief, and I asked Him to come and fill my life. I told God that I wanted to see people healed as well. I asked Him to allow me to flow in miracles." He went on to say, "I decided to step out and do as you told me to do. I started praying for everyone I could find who needed healing. It is amazing! I have seen so many people set free since then. Thank you so much for coming."

I was thrilled beyond words. I did not know that man's story until he told me about it. We touch people's lives in ways that we may never know until we step foot in eternity. Consider how many people may approach us in Heaven and say, "I have to tell you how you influenced me while we were on Earth. I'm here because of you." As Maximus Decimus Meridius said in the movie *Gladiator*, "What we do in life echoes in eternity."

Miracles are contagious. They ignite passion in others to go beyond a passive lifestyle. They reveal a loving, powerful God. A person does not have to minister perfectly to embark on this journey. They only need to embark.

Tears of Joy

There are some miracles that may seem small to others but huge to the one receiving them. Chronic pain is one of those types of miracles. Chronic pain is tiring both physically and emotionally, and God desires to lift that pain off of His children.

I had been invited to speak at a women's healing encounter in Youngstown, Ohio. The meeting was well attended by women who had come from many miles away to receive a miracle. After I preached about the woman with the issue of blood, I felt that the Lord wanted me to pray for people with pain in a shoulder. I invited them to come forward and began to pray for them one at a time. The Lord was moving in great power at that meeting, and the first few people I prayed for experienced healing as well as many other manifestations of the Holy Spirit. Some were overcome by the Spirit and fell to the ground. Some laughed, and some shook. As a result, the women responded with much faith and anticipation that they also would be healed. After I had prayed for a few women, I looked up and was shocked to see a long line of women in the center aisle of the church waiting for me to pray for them. One after another, I ministered to these women, and God was setting them free.

SHERRY EVANS

After I had prayed for the women for close to an hour, I saw a woman slowly and painfully hobbling to the front where I was standing. The look on her face gave away her pain. I felt great compassion for the woman, and I said to her, "Sit right down here on the front row, and I will pray for you. You don't have to stand any longer."

I asked her what was wrong, and she told me that she had pain in her hip. She explained that she could barely walk, sit or even sleep. The pain kept her awake night after night and inhabited her days. I felt even more compassion for her as I thought of her standing in that long line waiting to receive prayer. I also understood that she was desperate—desperate enough to continue standing in pain. She knew that Jesus was her Healer, and her faith helped her to persevere. I had preached Jesus as Healer that evening, and she was ready to receive from Him.

I asked the women who were sitting in the room watching the ministry to say with me, "This healing belongs to her because of what Jesus did." The woman with the hip pain also said, "This healing belongs to ME because of what Jesus did."

In this case, the miracle did not happen instantly, but after several commands and prayers, she began to cry. Then, with great emotion, she spoke out in between her tears. "Thank You, Jesus! Thank You! I love You! You are so good!" I praise You!" She openly and unashamedly cried and cried and cried.

"Ma'am, how are you feeling?" I asked. She ignored me and continued to cry and praise the Lord. I tried again. "Is there still some pain left? How are you?"

When I was finally able to get her attention, she said, "He removed all of my pain! It is all gone!" During the rest of the ministry time, she continued to cry and to speak aloud her praise to God for setting her free. She was in her own "glory bubble" with the Lord.

Moments like these can still bring happy, grateful tears to my eyes. We are blessed to be vessels that God flows through to bring healing and deliverance. We are truly privileged to have this honor and joy.

How Many Years?

I received a surprise one day when I checked my emails and found a message from a pastor of an older, denominational church. He wrote, "I am interested in having you come and speak in my church about healing." This was unusual in that this is a denomination that rarely practices healing ministry. I was quite intrigued and quickly emailed him back. At first, neither one of us had the financial means to make the visit happen. After a few emails, I forgot all about it.

Almost a year later, he sent me a new email. "We have the funds now. Will you come?" I was even more intrigued when I read his kind invitation. As is usual when I think about traveling in ministry, my heart began to beat a little bit faster in anticipation. I was excited, but I wanted to ask God if He wanted me to go. I told the pastor I would pray about it and get back to him.

I had many questions. Would I be able to minister freely? Did he really understand what I would be doing there? Would I unknowingly destroy his church?

The more I prayed the more I felt that God was in this. I remembered a prophetic word that I had received from a prophet named John Mark Pool. He had prophesied that I would go into older denominations and take the new things of the Spirit. I also recalled a word that I received from Apostle Bruce Ladebu saying that I was in the wrong place as a pastor. He said that I had a pioneering anointing. It was all fitting together, so I contacted the pastor of this church and told him that I would be honored to minister at his church. I was not disappointed. God had orchestrated the entire trip.

As I spoke about healing in the first meeting, I saw the "deer in the headlight" look on many people's faces. I knew all of this was new, different, and very, very strange. In spite of that, some did allow me to pray for them and some powerful miracles took place. A woman with Parkinson's disease stopped shaking. Several who came in with pain left without it. Then there were the emotional healings. A man was set free from severe anxiety, and a young woman was freed from deep depression. God was faithful to His Word.

At the next meeting, people knew what they were coming to hear and receive. After I preached, I offered to pray for people. These denominational folk came alive. One dear, elderly woman began to urge, "You have to go up and get prayer." She looked a little like the energizer bunny as she went from person to person, friend to friend, and encouraged them to allow me to pray for them.

I jokingly told her, "I'm taking you with me from now on while I travel."

She answered, "Yes! I would love that."

Many more miracles happened that night. God touched a child with severely limited sight. After prayer, she was able to see clearly what she only saw as shadows previously. There were those who had pain leave their bodies. I didn't know it that night, but there was one exciting miracle that remained unknown to me.

The next morning, I was scheduled to teach a healing class at the church. Before the meeting started, a man walked up to me and said, "May I speak to you sometime today?"

I said, "Sure," and went on with my class.

When we came to a break, the man walked up and said, "Is this a good time?"

I replied, "Yes, if it isn't too long."

"I wanted to tell you what happened last night," he said.

My interest was piqued then, and I told him, "Please do. What happened?"

He said, "When you were praying for other people, I was praying along with you." Many times when I minister, I ask the people to help by declaring certain things over those who are receiving prayer. He went on, "I noticed that, as I was doing this, the pain started leaving my knees, legs, hips, and feet. It was leaving without you praying for me at all. I had this terrible arthritis."

I was excited for him and said, "Wow! That is wonderful. God is so good."

He went on and said, "I woke up this morning with no pain in the lower half of my body. I got out of bed without any stiffness either. This was the first time I have been able to do this in fifty-two years."

I said, "What? How many years did you say?"

He repeated, "Fifty-two years!" Even I was amazed at this point.

Then he said, "I still have a little bit of pain in my shoulders and arms though."

Because I was teaching a class that day, I planned on having the participants pray for each other. I said, "Let's have someone in the class pray for you instead of me."

After the class was over, he came to me and said, "I did get prayer, and all of the pain is gone now. All of it!"

I was greatly blessed by this church. Their obedience to the Word was astounding. After I was done teaching, several people came to me and said, "Now that we know what the Bible teaches about healing, we are responsible to do this." This is a minister's dream response. I heard them speak with their pastor about how to incorporate healing ministry. Some talked of forming teams to go to homes to minister to the sick. I could barely believe what I was hearing.

SHERRY EVANS

I left that church with my heart full of gratitude to God. This assignment brought me great joy, and I left a part of my heart there. We truly have a good, good Father.

Miscellaneous Miracles

My Journey - Faithfulness Is Key

Years ago, I experienced much frustration when people were not healed as I prayed for them. What was I doing wrong? Should I even continue praying for the sick? I voiced my concerns quite often to a man, Roger Webb, who was mentoring me in the area of healing, and he advised me to study the subject of faithfulness in the Bible. That day, I looked up every verse I could find with the word faithfulness in it and asked the Holy Spirit to teach me about this important topic.

Later on that day, I decided to take a jog down my country road. It was warm, and I enjoyed every step along the way. I looked around at the beauty of God's creation, and I thought about how amazing God is. Suddenly, I became aware of how far I was able to jog in comparison to when I first began jogging earlier in the summer. I was jogging with little exertion or tiredness. It was then that I distinctly heard the Lord say, "Sherry, how did that happen?"

I knew the answer to that question. It happened because I had pushed myself to jog a little farther every single day.

The Lord continued to ask me questions. He asked, "Do you

remember the first time you ever preached?"

I answered, "Yes, it was so uncomfortable. Now it is easy for me."

The conversation went on. He asked, "What about when you first prayed for a sick person on Facebook? How was that?"

I answered, "Yes, I remember. I was nervous and unsure of what to say or do. It is extremely comfortable for me now."

Then He continued, "How about your first healing service? How did that go?"

I replied, "I was afraid no one would come, and I was concerned that no one would be healed. I don't have those fears any longer."

As the Lord asked me these questions, I began to understand faithfulness in a different light than I had previously. Faithfulness is more than just doing the same thing over and over again. Faithfulness is stretching into the new thing that the Lord has for you even when it is uncomfortable. If I had only jogged the same distance every day, I would not have advanced in my ability to jog longer distances. I had to purposely jog farther each time.

In the parable of the talents, those who gained additional talents took risks. (Matthew 25:14-30) They invested their talents instead of burying them. The "good and faithful" servants who took risks with their talents were rewarded with more talents. Even more importantly, they received the praise and commendation of the Master.

In the Bible, faith is compared to a mustard seed. Mustard seeds were the smallest of all seeds but grew to the largest of all herbs. When a person is faithful, faith continues to expand and grow. With increased faith, seeing miracles becomes commonplace. In Matthew 17:20, Jesus said, "…For truly I say unto you, 'If you have faith as a grain of mustard seed, you shall say to this mountain move from here to there, and it shall move. Nothing shall be impossible for you.'"

Take every opportunity to minister healing to those around you and do not shrink back from doing something new. Don't stop when you feel discouraged. Faith for healing is like a muscle. Your faith will grow as you continue to minister healing just as a muscle grows stronger when it is exercised.

An Amish Man and a Christmas Miracle

It was only a few weeks before Christmas when a young woman from my church called me on the phone and asked, "Would you please pray for my husband? When he was five years old, he was burnt over 95% of his body. He was actually not expected to live past the age of seventeen, but he is still here. The doctors told his parents that he needed repeated surgeries in order to provide him with skin grafts, but they didn't follow up on the surgeries. He is in so much pain."

I didn't completely understand the situation, so I asked, "What is causing the pain?"

She answered, "His skin is too tight, and he can't bend or move much in any direction." I asked her to call her husband to the phone so that I could pray for him directly. I could hear her calling her husband insistently several times.

Then I heard him say in an irritated voice, "What do you want?" Then all I heard were whispers between them. I could tell that he was reluctant to receive prayer by the length of time it took him to come to the phone.

When the man came to the phone, I asked him a few more questions. In answer, he explained, "I went in for a follow-up visit, and the doctors told me that I had to have surgery, but the chances of the surgery being successful are only 50%. They tell me I will be disabled for the rest of my life."

As I listened to him, much of his past behavior made more sense. He had seemed angry and depressed lately, and this was the reason why.

This man and his wife had formerly been Amish. It was difficult for them to leave their families and break away from their Amish culture. A woman from our church invited them to our services, and we quickly adopted this young couple as our own. After they began to attend our church, I was privileged to lead them both to the Lord. Because of their Amish background, they were just beginning to understand Jesus as their Healer.

I reminded him that Jesus paid for his healing before I prayed for him, and then I asked the Lord to supernaturally stretch the skin on his back. When I was done, I asked, "How is the pain level now?"

He was quiet for a moment, and then he answered with no expression in his voice, "I don't feel any pain."

I wondered if he were telling me the truth, so I said, "Try to find the pain. See if you can make it hurt again."

After a few minutes, he replied with no emotion, "Nothing makes it hurt now. I don't feel any pain." I got off of the phone still wondering if he was being honest with me.

It was a mild December that year, and I saw him a few days later outside of his workplace. I asked, "How is your back?" Instead of answering, he demonstrated. He bent all around with a big grin on his face. He bent back and forth and from side to side. I asked, "Is there any pain?"

He said, "No pain at all."

He could not move like that before I had prayed because of the tight skin. God had supernaturally stretched his skin. To this day, he has not had to have a surgery, and he still does not have any pain.

In a matter of a few months, this man experienced many new things. He learned to drive a car and use electricity. He bought his first Christmas tree and decorated it with lights. Most importantly, though, he came to know Jesus as both his Savior and his Healer. It was a Christmas that he will never forget.

Pain-free, Limp-free, Impediment-free

Try to imagine walking on a foot that has a nerve that is balled up and swollen. It's called a nerve tumor. On top of that, imagine having gout in your foot, a painful form of arthritis. If that wasn't enough, imagine you have bone-on-bone knee pain. Walking would be excruciating.

This was the condition of a woman brought to my home for prayer by her daughter. She slowly struggled up the steps to my front door. I could see the pain in her face.

I invited them in, and we chatted for a few minutes. The woman with the pain explained that she was scheduled for knee replacement surgery. With a tired voice, she told me about the gout, the nerve tumor, and how hard it was to walk. I explained to her that Jesus healed everyone who came to Him, and that He was well able and willing to heal her also.

As I began to pray, I asked the Holy Spirit to rest on her, and then I commanded the pain and the cause of the pain to go in Jesus' name. Immediately, she declared, "The pain is all gone." She seemed surprised and continued to move her leg around.

In order to test the pain level further, I said, "Walk around a little bit and see how it is feeling now."

She looked at me with a surprised look on her face, and said, "I don't feel any pain."

The woman and her daughter thanked me for the prayer and got up to go to their car. I walked with them down the steps, but this time the woman who previously had the pain walked much more quickly and easily than when she walked up them. When we got to the bottom of the steps, she turned to me and said, "I have no pain at all!" She sounded genuinely amazed.

The next day, I received an email from the woman's daughter. She wrote, "Not only does my mother have no pain in her feet or her knee, the nerve tumor itself is gone. It disappeared overnight. She is walking pain-free, limp-free, and impediment-free for the first time in twenty years!"

Since that time, she has become a member of the church that my husband and I pastor. She still has not had to have the knee replacement surgery, and the nerve tumor has not returned.

The gout flared up a few more times, but each time we prayed the pain left. The gout is now a thing of the past. If a symptom seems to come back after God healed it, affirm that Jesus is your Healer. Remind yourself, your body, and the enemy that by His stripes you were healed.

I'm Walking without Pain!

"Will you pray for me? I am in so much pain from a herniated disc." I woke up one morning to this message on Facebook. The woman explained to me that the disability was so great that she was unable to walk. If she wanted to get something to eat or if she needed to move anywhere, she had to wait until someone came to her home and lifted her out of the chair. She had to be carried wherever she needed to go. You can imagine her desperate feelings about this condition.

She continued to ask, "Would you pray for me on the phone?" I affirmed that I would, and she gave me her phone number.

I rang her number, and then I began by reminding her of what Jesus had done for her at the whipping post. He had paid the price for her healing. Then I prayed, "Lord, cause Your power to come on this woman. I release Your presence and fire to her." I sensed and felt the powerful presence of God manifesting in the room. After that, I spoke directly to the disc, saying, "In Jesus' name, disc, get back into place. All pain, go, and spine be completely healed."

"Can you tell if anything is happening?" I asked.

"The pain is lessening," she said in an excited voice. Sometimes, persistence is needed in healing, and this was one of those times. I prayed three or four times, and each time, the pain lessened until the pain was completely gone.

I said to her, "Do what you couldn't do before. Get up and walk." She threw her fear to the wind and gingerly got up from her chair. I could not see her, but I heard her clearly.

She said, "Wow! I'm walking without pain!" She chattered away to me for quite some time because she was so excited. As we hung up the phone, I quietly thanked God for what He had done.

Shortly after that, she went to her doctor for a new x-ray of her spine. After the x-ray was done, her doctor walked into the room where she was waiting and told her, "The disc is now in the correct place. Not only that, the disc is completely normal."

She boldly explained, "My God has healed me!"

Only God can put a disc back into place. What an awesome Father we have.

Hot Flashes, the Miracle Dog, and the "Drunk" Man

If you look around at all the animals, insects, and people that God created, you will know that He has a sense of humor. I'm sure that He often laughs with us and may sometimes even laugh at us.

On an ordinary day, as I was doing some work around the house, I heard the phone ring. I had no idea of the adventure that was to follow.

I picked the phone up to hear a man say, "Would you pray for my dog? Daisy, my dog, has not been able to walk for a while." I knew that the man really loved his dog. I also knew that this man had been having pain in his lungs, and that the doctors suspected cancer.

Even though I knew that the pain in his lungs was the more urgent need, I honored his request and prayed that God would touch Daisy. I prayed, "Lord, heal Daisy. I speak life to this dog, in Jesus' name." I prayed as quickly as I could and moved on to what I cared about more—the possible cancer in his lungs.

I asked, "Are you still having pain in your lungs?"

He said, "Well, yes, but I just called for you to pray for Daisy."

With a little bit of frustration, I said, "Well, may I pray for your lungs?"

He hesitated for a moment, but then he said, "OK."

I prayed a simple prayer of healing for his lungs, and then I heard his confused voice saying, "I'm having a hot flash! I didn't know that men could have hot flashes!"

I laughed and told him, "That is the power of God on you. That isn't a hot flash."

He sounded amazed as he exclaimed, "The pain is gone!"

At just that moment, his wife walked into the room, and I could clearly hear what she said. "Daisy just got up and walked! I can't believe it!" Then she loudly asked her husband, "WHAT ARE YOU DOING ON THE FLOOR, AND WHY ARE YOU ACTING DRUNK?"

By this time, I could barely contain my laughter. I knew that it was useless to try to explain to either one of them at that moment what was happening. I got off of the phone with a man thinking he was having a hot flash AND with no pain, his wife wondering why he was acting drunk, and a previously paralyzed dog walking normally.

When the man went back to the doctor's office for more tests, they found no cancer. The dog did well for a while and finally died. The husband got over his "hot flash".

Healing is serious. Many are desperate for a touch from God. However, it is also a great adventure. Many times, I have laughed as I watched God do the unusual. He surprises me and intrigues me. Ministering healing is far from boring. He truly is the most enjoyable Person I know.

Tingling in the Brain

I was surprised one day to receive a message on Facebook telling me that an old friend was in the hospital. She explained that she had been having terrible headaches that would not let up. After testing, the doctors discovered that she had hydrocephalus or fluid buildup in her brain. This is a serious condition that can be fatal if not properly treated. The treatment is normally surgery in which a shunt that drains the fluid into another part of the body is placed in the brain. Even after surgery, there are dangers of infection, mechanical failure or obstructions. Complete recovery is not always possible as brain damage can occur. She needed a miracle.

I called her on the phone the day before she was scheduled to have surgery to insert the shunt. I reminded her that Jesus was her Healer, and then I commanded the fluid to go from her brain. Even though I had a poor understanding of how hydrocephalus develops, I knew that God understood it all. He can easily go beyond my understanding.

She told me, "I feel tingling in my brain and head! I don't feel any more pain! The headache is gone!" The unrelenting pain disappeared as God touched her with His mighty power.

The next day, she told her doctor that she no longer had any pain. Since she was scheduled to have surgery that day, he was confused and decided to do a new scan on her brain. To the woman's delight, the scan showed that the fluid buildup was gone. There was no sign of the hydrocephalus anywhere in her brain.

Surgery was cancelled, and the woman had nothing left to do but to go home rejoicing. Several years have passed since that day, and she has not had another problem with hydrocephalus. Our powerful, healing God set her free.

The Persistent Mother (AKA Mama Bear) and the Prodigal Son

Have you prayed but the answer has not come yet? Don't give up. God loves persistence because it demonstrates faith and deep desire. I had a vivid and humorous experience that illustrated this principle.

A precious woman asked me if I would visit her son in jail. I live about an hour away, but I was quite willing to do this. She called the jail to see when the visiting hours were, and the officer told her that they were from 7:45 PM to 9 PM.

I arrived at the jail at about 7:55 PM only to hear a man standing at the door of the jail arguing with the officer inside. I won't repeat his language, but the end result was that they would not allow him in because he did not arrive before 7:50 PM.

I called the mom, who had not arrived yet, and explained the situation to her. She said, "Well, you just have to get in to see my son. Just wait until I get there." She pulled into a parking space near the jail and scurried up the steps to where I was standing. She hit the intercom button and said with an insistent tone of voice, "I am here to see my son."

The officer, who we could not see, said, "I'm sorry, but you must be here before 7:50 PM to enter."

The mother answered, "No, you don't understand. My friend is here. She is a pastor, and she came to pray for my son. She lives an hour away."

"Sorry, but you can't come in tonight. You can come tomorrow," the officer replied.

The mom continued to explain, "No, you don't understand. Tomorrow won't work. My friend is here. She is a pastor, and she came to pray for my son. She lives an hour away." She added, "This is so frustrating."

None of her persuasive words worked. The officer would not allow us in. She stood there a moment and decided to try again. She hit the intercom button forcefully, and when the officer answered, she began the same line of reasoning. "My friend is here. She is a pastor, and she came to pray for my son. She lives an hour away. Is there anything you can do?"

The officer explained, "I'm sorry, but there is no one downstairs to let you in. You cannot come in."

I felt a little embarrassed and whispered to her, "I'll come back tomorrow." She would hear nothing of it. She was determined to get me in that night.

The mom (AKA Mama Bear) thought a few more moments and said, "I know what I'll do. I'll call the police chief." She knew that he was not in the office at that time of night, and, in fact, would be at home trying to relax. In the past, when she tried to call him after his work hours, he never answered. This time, he did answer.

When she had the police chief on the phone, she said with a frustrated voice, "They won't let me in to see my son." Of course, he explained to her what she already knew. He told her that she had to be there before 7:50 PM. Mama Bear went into the same explanation that she had given to the officer in the jail. "YOU DON'T UNDERSTAND. MY FRIEND IS HERE. SHE IS A PASTOR, AND SHE CAME TO PRAY FOR MY SON. SHE LIVES AN HOUR AWAY." I could tell that the police chief was trying to reason with her, but her mind was made up.

He sighed and said, "OK. I'll call the warden and see what I can do."

A few minutes later, the police chief called her back and told her that the warden insisted that it was impossible for us to get in that night. The mom politely, but urgently, continued to speak with the police chief, using the same reasoning as before. "MY FRIEND IS HERE, SHE IS A PASTOR, AND SHE CAME TO PRAY FOR MY SON. SHE LIVES AN HOUR AWAY." By this time, I was really embarrassed. I couldn't believe what I was hearing.

After a time, she simply wore that police chief down. He finally said with an exasperated voice, "Who is the officer that you were talking to on the intercom?"

At that point, the mom hit the intercom button insistently. Again, the officer came on and said, "May I help you?"

Mom said, "What's your name? I have the police chief on the phone." I would have loved to have seen the police officer's face. I can imagine him rolling his eyes in frustration. The officer told her his name, and she relayed the information to the chief. The police chief told her that he would see if he could do anything.

A few minutes later, the chief called back and said, "Ma'am, they are going to send someone down to let you in." Triumph!

True to his word, an officer came down and impatiently let us in. He glared at us and said, "From now on, you have to be here before 7:50 PM."

I entered a room where I was separated from the young man by a glass panel, and picked up the phone to speak to him. After a few questions about how he was, I asked him, "What are your concerns tonight?"

He looked down and spoke so quietly that I could barely hear him. "I feel like a failure. Everyone has given up on me, and I wonder if I should even go on."

I spoke to him about Jesus and His ability to take those who have failed in some way and to make them powerful men and women of God. I used Peter as an example. God had not given up on him. Even though he could not look at me, I could see tears coming to this man's eyes. I added, "Your mother just fought and fought and fought to get us in to see you tonight. She has definitely not given up on you." He looked up at me in surprise and, for the first time that night, smiled widely.

"How is your relationship with God?" I asked.

He answered sadly, "Not good. I walked away from God. I'm not worthy of Him."

I gently replied, "None of us are worthy of God. Without Jesus, we are all equally unworthy. With Jesus, we are all equally worthy." I reminded this man of what Jesus did for him on the cross.

Then I asked, "Are you ready to recommit your life to the Lord? He loves you and is waiting for you with open arms."

Through his tears, he said, "Yes, I am."

As we prayed, the intense presence of God filled the room. I prayed that every addiction would be broken off of him and that God would fill him with His Spirit. I released peace and asked the Lord to strengthen him and give him wisdom. He had a toothache, and, as I commanded it to go, every bit of pain left. Because of this mother's persistence and desperation, her son made a new commitment to the Lord and was touched by His power.

Several months later, the persistent mother attended one of our Thursday night services. She raised her hand and asked if she could share a testimony. With joy, she explained that her son was out of jail now, was clean from drugs, and was working at a good job.

There is a parable in Luke 18 about a judge who did not want to be bothered by a widow woman. Even though the judge did not care about her, she wore him out with her persistence, and, as a result, she received what she needed.

God is not an unjust judge. He is a loving Father. However, there are times when we must persist in coming to Him with a need. Luke 18:7 and 8 says, "And shall not the Lord avenge His own elect that cry out to Him day and night, though He has been long suffering with them? I say to you, He will avenge them speedily. Yet when the Son of Man comes, will He find faith on the earth?"

When you want to give up, remember this mom fighting to see her son. Be persistent. This is a season in which persistence in prayer is important. What promise in the Word are you standing on? What has God put in your heart to believe for? Whom are you praying for to receive deliverance or salvation? Are you crying out to God for a new awakening on this earth? How much do you want it?   Delays are not denials. Your faith will bring victory to many. Don't give up.

The "Spring Chicken"

I decided to attend a revival service at an area church one summer evening with a deep desire for God to touch me. As I drove to the service, anticipation filled my heart, but I didn't know that God had something very special for me that night that involved another person.

As I walked into the church and found a seat, I overheard a woman speak to herself and to God, saying, "Oh, Lord, my feet hurt so bad!" Immediately, I felt compassion for this woman. She was a short, elderly woman with a long dress on, and she was sitting in the row right in front of me. It was a setup from God from the very beginning.

I wanted to offer to pray for her, but I was uncomfortable doing so without permission from the pastor. I began to pray, "Lord, should I minister to her here? I'm a visitor in this church, and no one knows me." I looked around and realized that the pastor was not there yet. I could not even ask him.

After thinking about it for a few minutes, I decided that, out of respect for the pastor, I would not pray for her. I was disappointed, but I felt confident that I had made the right decision. I silently asked the Lord to make a way for me to minister to her, and then I settled down to enjoy the service. During the meeting, my thoughts kept drifting to the pain that she was in.

After the meeting, I walked towards the door of the church to go home, and I wistfully thought about the woman with the painful feet. Oh, how I wished I would have been able to pray for her. When I opened the door to go outside, my heart did a few flip flops, and I stepped back in amazement. Standing right there outside the door was that woman. The church had been packed that night. I knew that this could not be a coincidence. The Lord had created an opportunity for me to pray for her in a way that would not be disrespectful to the pastor of the church. All I could think about was how great God is. Only He could have arranged this.

I said to her, "Ma'am, you don't know me, but I overheard you when you said that your feet hurt. How do your feet feel now?"

"Oh, they still hurt so bad. I have diabetic pain." She spoke in a labored voice. I thought of how this woman loved God so much that she wanted to be in church, even with this pain.

I asked, "May I pray for your feet? I know you don't know me, but I'm a believer in Jesus like you are. He paid for your healing. It belongs to you right now. Jesus healed everyone who came to Him, so I know that He wants to heal you as well."

"Oh, yes, please," she said, "we are sisters in Christ. I would love for you to pray for me."

As I laid hands on her, I commanded the neuropathy pain to go and spoke healing to her feet. Then I waited to see how she was feeling. Suddenly, she began to act like a young woman who had just won the lottery. She danced and stomped her feet while she shouted, "I'm healed! I'm healed! Jesus healed me!" Then she danced and stomped her feet some more. It would be an understatement to say that she was excited. The joy of the Lord was all over her.

Just then, a man drove up in a car to pick her up. She no longer walked with a slow, labored gait. Instead, she walked to that car like a spring chicken. There was a bounce in her step and a grin on her face. She looked back at me with a surprised expression and shouted, "Hey, I can even walk without a limp!"

What a wonderful Father! He gave me the desire of my heart and gave the woman a miracle all at the same time.

Ministering Healing

The Practical Side

Learning to minister healing is a journey. The Holy Spirit will personally mentor those who embark on this journey. Not everyone will minister healing in exactly the same way because the Holy Spirit is creative. He will vary His approach according to a person's primary gifting and personality. However, there are principles that remain the same for everyone. In addition, just as it is helpful to have training wheels to learn to ride a bike, so it is helpful to have "training wheels" or suggestions when learning to pray for the sick.

As in all ministries, it is important to see each person as one who is deeply loved by God. Be considerate and loving in your approach. Begin by asking the person about their need. Is there pain? Where is the pain located? Has a doctor diagnosed the cause of the pain? It is not necessary to know every detail because God knows the details, but a few questions may help you understand how to pray.

Remind the person receiving prayer that Jesus healed everyone who came to Him when He was on Earth. Jesus is the same now as He was then. He always did the will of the Father, so you can rest assured that it is always God's will to heal. Remind the person you are praying for that it is impossible to earn healing. It has already been paid for at the whipping post. Jesus heals because of His great love and compassion. He does not need any other reason.

Lay hands on the person needing healing in a place that is appropriate. You may need to ask permission to lay hands on people who are unfamiliar with the process of healing. It is not necessary to touch a person in order to minister healing, however. Healing can take place over the phone or through a text message as well.

Focus on the Holy Spirit inside of you. When I began to minister in the area of healing, I would sometimes focus on myself. I would think about how many people I had seen healed with that particular disease. Those types of thoughts bring doubt and failure. Jesus healed all types of diseases, He has not changed, and He lives inside of you and I. Self-focus is like pulling out the plug from the source of the power. The power flows from the Lord inside of you. Stay plugged into the power source through focusing on Him.

As you begin to pray, remember that you are one with Christ. You are not performing for Him, but instead you are ministering with Him. Allow Him to flow through you to others.

If you feel fear, remember that the Word says that "Perfect love casts out fear." (I John 4:18) I have learned to counter fear by thinking about God's love for the person who needs healing. As I think of God's love, love begins to rise up in my heart towards that person as well. Love casts out the fear of failure or making a mistake. In addition, God's love does not ebb and flow according to your success rate in seeing the sick healed. We are secure in His love.

I am often asked, "But what do I say when ministering healing?" What you say is not nearly as important as putting your trust in the Healer. God can and will heal in response to faith, not according to the perfection of your prayer. When I began ministering in healing, I experimented. Sometimes I commanded healing. Sometimes I would say, "Lord, cause Your power to go through this person and heal them." At other times, I laid hands on the person needing healing without saying a word. Occasionally, I would ask them to move the part of their body that needed to be healed. I found that, unless the Lord gave me a definite way to minister, it did not matter what I said. It was faith that brought the healing.

After you have prayed, ask the person to report what is happening in their body. Is the pain less, the same or more? Is anything else unusual happening? Do they feel heat or tingling anywhere in their body? Sometimes, they may also feel cold, numbness or pressure when God is healing them. Many people will not feel anything at all even though God is bringing the healing. Do not become concerned about a lack of manifestations.

If the pain is not completely gone, pray again. Continue praying until the pain is no longer present, the person wants you to stop or there is no more progress. It is not uncommon to need to pray more than once for healing to manifest. Don't get in a hurry out of nervousness. Rest in Him.

Follow the lead of the Holy Spirit. If you are praying for one thing and the person is feeling heat or tingling in another part of their body, begin to focus on ministering to that area. The Holy Spirit knows what He is doing.

If the pain intensifies, or if the person feels a sudden headache, a new pain or nausea, they may need deliverance from a spirit of infirmity or pain. Often, it leaves on its own, but if it does not, you may need to command it to go in the powerful name of Jesus.

If nothing appears to be happening, remember that only a miracle is instant. Healing is gradual. I have seen healing manifest the next hour, the next day or even a week later. Simply tell the person who needs healing to continue to trust and thank God for healing them. Keep your faith anchored in the power of God. You did your part. Trust God to do His part.

If the healing has manifested, explain what to do if the pain tries to come back. Tell them that they keep their healing the same way that they have received their healing—through faith in Jesus as Healer. Remind them to affirm that Jesus IS their Healer and tell them to command that pain or sickness to go in His name.

After each healing encounter, give the situation to the Lord. If they were healed, thank God. If the healing did not manifest yet, give it to God. Then pray for the next person. Out of love, we lay down our lives to see the next person healed, and then the next person, and then the next person.

Relax. Put more trust in Jesus' ability to heal than in your ability to heal. Rest in Him. Have fun. Yes, healing is serious, but ministering with the Holy Spirit is a great adventure. Don't wait. Start now.

Developing a Culture for the Supernatural Church

I believe that God has a dream for His church. He envisions a group of people that loves Him supremely and pursues Him passionately. In like manner, He desires a body of believers that can minister His love to others through the demonstration of His power. Jesus longs for all to be healed and set free, and He paid a tremendously high price for our healing. The provision has been made through the stripes on His back. Now He calls us to enforce the victory that He paid for. Unfortunately, many have sold out for so much less than what God designed for us to walk in.

Our churches should all reflect the ministry of Jesus on Earth, which included healing. Many have wondered how to develop a miracle healing culture in the church. The Lord spoke to me directly concerning this issue in a vivid dream.

In my dream, a mother brought her son to me and asked me to pray for his healing. Even though it is not necessary to be in a church to heal the sick, in my dream I decided to go to a church building.

I saw a huge building that I knew was a church down the road from where I was standing. I directed the young man and his mother to follow me to the massive building. We walked over to the church and, as I got closer, I noticed how modern it looked. It appeared to me to resemble a large corporation building with many windows. We continued to the door and saw an escalator going to the top floor. As we went up the escalator, I looked around at the people moving up and down on the escalator. Everyone seemed consumed with their own affairs. I saw men in suits talking on their phones, and I knew in my dream that they were making business deals.

When we reached the top floor, I looked around in shock at what I saw. The room was full of people, but none of them seemed to notice us. I again noticed that the men were all on their phones making deals. The teenagers were talking with each other with whispers and giggles.

I noticed a worship team in the front of the room. They were not worshiping, however. They seemed to be providing background noise or perhaps entertainment. No one in the room was worshiping either. They were too busy making deals or socializing with their friends.

Then I saw him. There was a man standing to the side who looked like a dishonest salesperson. He had a sly look on his face and was wearing extravagantly expensive clothing. As he stood there, he twirled his mustache around with his finger. I realized that this was the "Jesus" that the people in the room worshiped. He was not the true Jesus, but it was THEIR Jesus.

In dismay, I continued to look around at the scene. I sadly told the young man and his mother, "I can't pray for your healing here." We left in disappointment.

We headed back down the escalator and exited the building. I looked around wondering what I should do next. Then I noticed a smaller, enclosed porch off of the top floor of the large building. I told the young man and his mother, "Let's try that porch."

I realized that there was a separate door and stairway to get to the top to where the porch was. There was no elevator. Instead, we would need to climb the stairs. As we approached the stairs, I noticed that we needed to go through a deep river in order to get to the steps.

The three of us walked through the river and then walked up the steps. What a difference between the porch and the large building we had already been in. As we entered the enclosed porch, we were warmly greeted by those in the room. There were far less people in this room than in the large corporate building room, but they were filled with warmth and love. They surrounded us with faces full of concern.

There was no worship team in the room, but I knew that the people were worshiping in their hearts. I sensed the presence of God all around.

Then I saw HIM! I saw Jesus standing there with a huge smile on His face. Love radiated from Him, and He welcomed us with open arms. He did not have expensive clothing on, but He was glorious in every way.

My heart jumped with joy. I knew that this was the place in which I would pray for this young man, and he would be healed. Then I woke up.

The Lord wanted me to understand where my healing ministry would thrive, as well as to know how to develop a supernatural culture in the church. There are several areas to consider.

The Focus

The focus of the people in the corporate-type building was purely on themselves or their friends. A false Jesus was there, but they did not appear to see Him. The people were more interested in "getting a good deal in life" than worshiping the King of Kings and Lord of Lords.

The focus of the people on the porch was Jesus. It was obvious that they were in love with Him. They seemed utterly abandoned to Him. There was an unspoken fellowship that took place between the people and Jesus.

If we wish to have a culture of the supernatural in our churches we need to fall in love with Jesus. He must be more to us than a means to get ahead in life. Our focus must be on Him and His heart for those who are lost and suffering. Our worship must be from the heart. The supernatural church must be willing to lay down their comfort and self-interest in order to embrace the Lord's interests.

Their Love

In the corporate building, the lost and the least were ignored. The young man and his mother did not fit in with the people in the building, so they were overlooked. It appeared that the people had no time to reach out to the "outcasts".

On the porch, we were embraced warmly. The people reflected the love of the Lord they adored. They truly cared about the needs of the young man and his mother.

In order to have a culture of healing, we need to cultivate a love for people. The Bible says that Jesus moved with compassion when He healed the sick. We must also have that compassion within us for the sick and suffering. Compassion will cause us to take time for those in our midst who are different or in need.

Their "Jesus"

Those in the corporate building were looking for a "Jesus" who would help them get ahead in life but would ask very little more of them. Their "Jesus" was just a small addition to their already busy lives.

Those on the porch had a deep relationship with a loving Jesus who was intricately involved in their lives. They had obviously laid down their lives for this One who they loved so much.

In developing a supernatural culture, there needs to be an accurate depiction of Jesus. He is the way, the truth, and the life. (John 14:6) We follow His example of how to minister healing. Our relationship with Him must be deep and personal. We need to allow Him to be the center of everything that happens in our gatherings and allow Him to minister as He desires.

The Lord is developing churches and groups such as the "porch folk". Healing will become more and more commonplace in these places. We have much to look forward to because our best days as a church are still ahead of us. Our preparation is underway.

Pick up Your Shoes

This is truly a time in which God is forming an army of fire-filled believers to preach the gospel and heal the sick. However, it has not been without opposition. I have often asked groups of believers what is keeping them from moving forward in healing, and the most frequent answer I have received is fear.

I had a dream years ago in which my husband and I were on a mission trip. I knew in my dream that this was a dangerous trip. One morning, our group was in a large room waiting for our host and hostess to arrive, but they did not come at the time they were scheduled to come. I quickly became concerned because I knew that this trip was risky, and I was concerned for their welfare.

Suddenly, the door banged open and a man came in. He breathlessly shouted, "YOU HAVE TO GET OUT OF HERE RIGHT NOW!" Everyone began to run out the door.

I remembered that I had shoes on the floor beside me, and I picked the two pairs up that I owned so that I could take them with me. Then I looked around and was amazed to see that there were shoes still on the floor all over the room. It appeared that no one had picked up their shoes.

I saw a friend's pair of extra shoes beside me and I picked them up. I thought that I could take them for her. I tried to carry my shoes and her shoes out the door, but I realized that I wasn't going to be able to take hers and mine at the same time. *If she doesn't care enough to take her own shoes, I can't take them for her*, I thought. I quickly put her shoes down and headed for the open door.

I watched as people around me were running as if in a panic. Soon, we came to a building that held our suitcases. In my dream, I understood that I was going to need my suitcases for the next mission trip I went on. I knew that there were supplies stored in them for these trips.

I watched as everyone ran right by the building that housed the suitcases. They were too afraid to stop long enough to get what belonged to them. Then I saw one woman stride over to the building, her arms swinging by her side. As soon as I saw her determination to get what belonged to her, I decided that I would not allow fear to stop me from getting my supplies either. I marched over towards the building with a determined look on my face.

As I was approaching the building, some children came out carrying our suitcases for us. They were laughing and singing with their childlike voices. They sang, "Here's your stuff! These are for you!" Then I woke up.

The Lord spoke to me and explained that the shoes that were left behind were gifts and callings. His people were allowing fear to stop them from what He had called them to walk in.

All believers can minister healing, but many live in fear of making a mistake or failing to see someone healed. These were "shoes" that were being left behind.

I could not pick up my friend's shoes because I already had my hands full with my own. The Lord showed me that each one of us must walk in our own gifts and callings or there will be people unreached. We are needed—every one of us.

On top of that, many were allowing fear to stop them from getting their "suitcases". These held the necessary equipment from the Lord that is needed to do the work of the ministry.

The best part of the dream was the childlike joy that was illustrated as I went to get my suitcases. The children exuded joy as they brought out our suitcases. There is great joy for those who refuse to allow fear to stop them from getting what the Lord has for them. I can testify to that joy.

Don't leave your shoes behind out of fear. The world needs you and the One who is inside of you. There are people who only you can reach. There are people near you who need a healing touch that only you can provide. You can be sure that the joy of the Lord will be your strength.

Lord, I pray that a supernatural power and boldness will come upon each person reading this book. Make them miracle workers. Give them a determination to walk in all that You have for them. Fill them with FIRE, Lord. May they know Your joy in them as they go. Thank You, Lord. In Jesus' name, amen.

Prayer for Healing

Imagine that you are sitting amongst the multitudes when Jesus was on Earth. He looks right at you and asks you to come to Him. He speaks to the sickness and disease in your body and commands it to go from you. You are healed! As you read the prayer that follows, rest in His love and His healing touch in your life.

Lord, thank You for the price that You paid for our healing. Right now, cause Your mighty power and healing fire to go through bodies. In Jesus' name, I speak to every spirit of infirmity to go from them. I command pain to disappear and the causes of the pain to be healed. Arthritis, you must go. Chronic headaches, you must stop. Tumors, shrink and disappear in Jesus' name. Cancer, diabetes, and every disease that has a name, bow to the name of Jesus. Fibroids, shrink and leave. Lord, give people dental miracles. Every organ be restored and healed in Jesus' name. Lord, lay Your hand on each one of them. Thank You, Lord! In Jesus' name, amen.

About The Author

Sherry Evans has a passion to see Jesus receive what He paid for at the cross. She endeavors to accomplish this through a three-fold mandate—demonstration of God's healing power, impartation of God's grace and fire, and equipping the body of Christ through teaching and preaching. Sherry desires to see the church in revival and the lost saved. She holds revival and healing services, as well as healing classes, in various churches and other venues. She also is currently the co-pastor of Covenant Church in Jefferson, OH, along with her husband, Bill.

Contact Information

www.FireReach.com
sherryevans1280@yahoo.com

Deeper Life Press

www.findrefuge.tv

Made in the USA
Middletown, DE
05 September 2024